INCENTIVE PAY

Michael Cannell is a Manpower Adviser at the National Economic Development Office, having previously worked for ACAS and the TUC. Recent projects include helping to introduce team working (and to change pay systems) in the UK garment industries, and the forthcoming NEDO/IPM book on skills-based pay.

Dr Stephen Wood is Senior Lecturer in Industrial Relations at the London School of Economics and Joint Editor of the *British Journal of Industrial Relations*. His books include *The Transformation of Work?*, *The Car Industry* (with D. Marsden *et al.*) and *Recruitment and Selection in the Labour Market* (with P. Windolf). His most recent work has been on the development of human resource management and changing payment systems in British manufacturing.

Michael Cannell and Stephen Wood

INCENTIVE PAY
impact and evolution

Institute of Personnel Management
and
National Economic Development Office

Typeset by Mendip Communications Ltd, Frome, Somerset and printed in Great Britain by The Cromwell Press, Wiltshire

British Library Cataloguing in Publication Data

Cannell, Michael
    Incentive Pay: Impact and Evolution
    I. Title II. Wood, Stephen
    331.2

ISBN 0–85292–490 9

The views expressed in this book are the authors' own, and may not necessarily reflect those of the IPM or NEDO.

Contents

List of tables

vi

List of tables

List of illustrations

About NEDO

The National Economic Development Council brings together representatives of Government, management, the trade unions and other interests to assess economic performance and opportunities for improving it. The Council meets quarterly, under the chairmanship of the Chancellor of the Exchequer and other Secretaries of State.

There are eighteen sector groups and working parties covering different parts of industry or working on practical industrial issues. The sectors covered include construction, electronics, engineering, and tourism and leisure. Working parties are studying biotechnology, water effluent treatment technology, and the European public sector market.

The National Economic Development Office supports the work of the Council and its sector groups and working parties. It carries out independent research and provides advice on ways of improving economic performance, competitive power and the efficiency of industry, stimulating new ideas and practical action.

Foreword

In Europe, the Americas and the countries of the Pacific rim competition is driving forward efforts to improve quality and productivity. The effects are widespread. Organizations in the forefront, in the public as well as the private sector, are finding that efficiency and customer service are becoming essential objectives. In these circumstances growing emphasis is being placed on the contribution individuals can make to performance. It is crucial that employers convey the right messages to people about the ways they can help competitiveness and that they ensure that such messages are correctly understood.

Pay provides a key line of communication with employees. Profit-related pay has grown dramatically in recent years, and the use of performance-related pay is becoming more widespread for people at all levels. This book examines employers' experience with incentive pay and shows how important it is to find a pay system which works for each organization. All pay systems have drawbacks as well as positive qualities, and without careful management and regular review the flaws in a system can get out of hand without anyone realizing what is happening. This book shows that the better employers do not get caught out in this way; they plan, monitor and evaluate, and seek to match their pay systems to the needs of their organization.

The work which has gone into this book has been carried out jointly by the National Economic Development Office and the Institute of Personnel Management. It will be followed shortly by another jointly published volume, on skills-based pay.

WALTER ELTIS, Director General
National Economic Development Office

ROGER FARRANCE, President
Institute of Personnel Management

Acknowledgements

The review of settlements between 1983 and 1991, as reported in Incomes Data Service reports, was carried out by Jo Poke, Assistant Librarian, IPM. The questionnaire survey was conducted by Phil Long, the IPM's Manager – Research. Dr Alex Bowen, Head of Policy, Analysis and Statistics, Economic and Statistics Division, NEDO, provided information on and analyses from the New Earnings Survey.

The authors are grateful to those who helped to make this book possible by being interviewed or completing the IPM/NEDO questionnaire, and to all the members of the Incentive Pay Steering Group listed in Appendix 3. Especial thanks are due to John Stevens and Richard Coles for their helpful suggestions on structure and drafts, and to Simone Day for word-processing countless drafts.

Material from *Does Performance Pay Motivate?* (Inland Revenue Staff Federation, 1991) by Dr David Marsden and Dr Ray Richardson is reproduced with their kind permission; extracts from the PRP Report No. 4 (1990) are reproduced with the permission of LACSAB.

Introduction

Looking back on the 1980s, the most often reported development on the pay front was the introduction or extension of performance-based pay for managers and other white-collar workers, usually linked to some kind of appraisal of performance. There were also a few frequently quoted examples of performance-related pay on the shop floor. It appeared that traditional piece-rate schemes for manual workers were in decline, and that profit-related pay was growing.

But there was little hard evidence to back these impressions. It therefore appeared to the IPM and NEDO that the time was ripe to find out what was really happening, in both the public and the private sectors. It seemed clear that employers and other parties, including trade unions, could benefit from such information when considering the amendment of existing payment systems or the introduction of new ones.

The research

The terms of reference for the joint research project were to examine the extent and nature of individual and group incentive payment systems at all levels of employee; to consider recent developments, sometimes in the context of innovative working methods; and to assess the efficacy of such systems in terms of recruitment, retention and the acquisition of new skills. This involved a number of different stages. Approximately 3,000 settlements described in the Incomes Data Services (IDS) reports from January 1982 to March 1991 were examined, as were the trends since the mid-1970s revealed by the New Earnings

Survey (NES). In early 1991 a questionnaire survey (subsequently referred to as 'the survey') was conducted among a broad cross-section of public and private organizations. (For further details of survey sample and methodology, see Appendix 2.) This was followed by face-to-face interviews with personnel managers from forty-four organizations identified as having made interesting recent changes in their payment systems.

The research project considered payment systems aimed at improving individual or group performance which have traditionally been introduced mainly to *motivate* employees to increase output. Despite the questions this book raises about their *success* in motivating people, therefore, the term 'incentive pay' has been used as a generic term for individual and group payment by results schemes (PBR), performance-related pay (PRP), and profit-related pay; a full set of definitions appears in the glossary. Unless otherwise stated, results shown in all figures and tables are derived from the new IPM/NEDO research.

Structure of the book

After an initial look at the overall context and how pay has been influenced by environmental factors (Chapter 1), the book describes recent developments in the three main categories of incentive pay: individual payment by results (Chapter 2); group performance-related pay, including in particular profit-sharing (Chapter 3); and individual performance-related pay (Chapters 4–5) which, because of its recent growth and because up to now there have been only limited attempts to assess it, receives extensive consideration. The book ends with general conclusions from the preceding chapters, which it is hoped will help to give a framework for those reviewing existing pay systems or introducing new systems.

In Chapters 2, 3 and 4 consideration of developments begins by looking at recent history as revealed by the IDS reports and the statistical data from the NES and the present survey. Most of the material for the report is, however, drawn from the interviews. Readers will bear in mind that, by the very nature of pay, and particularly because it is virtually impossible to compare different types of pay system side by side in the same establishment to provide a controlled experiment, there can be no such thing as absolute objectivity in assessing the effectiveness of various types of pay system. There is no substitute for the views of people with experience, and extensive use is therefore made of quotations from those with whom discussions were held. This material is supported by case studies, chosen to illustrate particular themes. There have been few recent published studies on this subject, including PRP, but where it exists relevant work has been drawn upon.

The focus on PRP

Although the book looks at three types of what is being called 'incentive pay' (group performance-related pay, individual PBR and PRP), these different categories do not receive equal treatment in terms of space. Discussion of PRP accounts for more than half the book, first because its growth was the most significant factor on the pay scene in the 1980s, and it appears likely to increase. Second, as enthusiasm for PRP spreads, there is greater questioning of it. This comes not only from trade unions, as PRP is introduced into unionized environments, but from managers. Thirdly, PRP purports to be about a great deal more than motivation; it is part and parcel of the change in management philosophy which has taken place during the last decade. For all these reasons it merits substantial consideration.

1

The overall context

The past thirty years have seen some fundamental shifts in the types and mix of jobs in the economy. Just as fundamentally, the nature of competition has altered and become much more intense. Both these changes have been accompanied by changing fashions in pay systems. The ways in which people are paid have often developed haphazardly, with different schemes being introduced for different sets of people at different times and with different motives. In some occupations and some industries there have been radical changes in jobs and pay systems, but in others long-standing pay systems persist with little change. Although there have been enormous advances in technology, particularly automation, there are still a significant number of repetitive jobs with a high labour content, for example in garment and footwear manufacturing, where piecework incentive systems are still relatively common.

The 1950s saw the spread of piecework as techniques of work measurement were refined to set performance standards for less repetitive tasks; this process continued and eventually peaked in the early 1980s. But as piecework moved into areas of less repetitive work, such as short batch production, other approaches to pay were being developed, such as measured daywork. Moving into the 1980s, with a growing emphasis on quality and 'right first time', the problems associated with highly repetitive tasks began to be recognized and there were moves to stimulate commitment and interest by giving people broader and more rewarding jobs by, for example, the introduction of team working. Pay became related more to the total job than to elements of the job, and the individual's responsibility for quality started to be formally recognized in other ways than by simply imposing pay penalties for re-work.

During the 1970s attention had turned towards greater emphasis on pay for white-collar workers. This trend was reinforced by the growth of jobs in the service sector. Work output was more difficult to measure in a non-manufacturing setting, and this called for a new approach to incentive pay. A large number of white-collar workers were on incremental payment systems based on the belief that the contribution of white-collar workers increased with experience, and it was therefore appropriate to pay more as their length of service increased. To relate effort, qualifications and other aspects of jobs more clearly to pay, job evaluation systems were often introduced.

An accelerating rate of change and the search for savings in 'non-productive' jobs during the 1980s often made it difficult to maintain highly analytical systems with detailed job descriptions and job evaluation committees. Simultaneously the changing social climate put greater emphasis on individualism. The emphasis has shifted from analysis of job content and effort (inputs) to individual achievement (outputs). Pay systems have reflected this, although because changes have occurred gradually many organizations still have a variety of payment systems.

Payment systems and changes to them are products of a changing environment. Piece-rate pay systems were linked with manufacturing philosophies prevailing at the time. The current decline of individual PBR and the rise of PRP and profit-related pay are linked with the management preoccupations of the moment: for example, improvements in quality, the development of just-in-time manufacturing, greater focus on the customer, decentralization of businesses, flatter organizational structures and increases in individual accountability. These changing influences on pay can be listed in terms of movement:

From	Towards
Limited competition	More intense competition
Standardized work	Flexibility
Standard products	Innovation
Long runs	Short runs
Product-driven systems	Customer-driven systems
Quantity	Quality
Individual output	Team working
Fixed tasks	Continuous improvement
Re-work	'Right first time'
Making for stock	Just-in-time
Being told what to do	Involvement
Skills for life	New skills
Jobs for life	Less security
Measuring output	Appraising contribution
Rewarding seniority	Rewarding achievement
Job-based systems	People-based systems

These considerations are not limited to the private sector or to manufacturing or service industries, and are making an impact in the public sector too.

It is interesting to note that the preoccupation with pay systems is a feature of life in the UK and the USA. There seems to be more stability of approach in the rest of Europe and in Japan, although this suggestion is based on anecdotal rather than empirical evidence. In the UK the next stage may be greater attention to careers and the development of skills. The importance of developing people on a broader basis to meet the unpredictable challenges of the future is increasingly being recognized.

In some organizations there has been a move towards systems that reward individuals for acquiring new skills – in other words, pay systems that not only reward individuals for their contribution today but set out the rewards for their potential contribution tomorrow. Against this is the nagging suspicion harboured by some that the complexities of many incentive and skill-based systems are themselves counterproductive and that, looking to Europe and Japan for examples, given the right culture, incentives could be superfluous and might be abandoned.

The aims of pay systems have widened in line with the changing circumstances and philosophies mentioned above. Whereas pay systems were once probably designed to do nothing more than motivate, reward, recruit and retain employees, they now have wider expectations thrust upon them: improving quality and skills, changing the work culture and promoting co-operation are now included in their possible aims, which can be summarized as:

- *To increase effort:* motivation and reward.
- *To compete in the labour market:* recruitment and retention.
- *To improve quality:* right first time and continuous improvement.
- *To change culture:* innovation and customer service.
- *To promote co-operation:* team working.
- *To improve skills and flexibility:* upgrading competence and personal development.

The extent to which the new pay systems have met these expectations provides some of the themes for this book. It also provides a link with the companion volume, on skills-based pay, to be published by NEDO and the IPM in the near future.

2

The decline of piecework

Although its origins are much older, modern developments in piecework were closely linked to the ideas of
F. W. Taylor, who argued that every manufacturing operation could be broken down by work study in the interests
of efficiency. The object of piece rates was therefore to
reward the input of labour to closely defined tasks and, by
doing so, to stimulate people to work at a faster pace with
increased concentration, thus producing a larger output of
manufactured goods. In the United Kingdom piecework
probably enjoyed its greatest popularity as a concept in the
1950s or even earlier; by the early 1960s authors like
Wilfred Brown (1962) were making telling criticisms of it,
although its use continued to grow into the 1980s.

Nevertheless piecework survives, and some industries,
such as clothing, footwear and construction, remain heavily reliant on it. It is also well entrenched in some parts of
the public sector. However, the survey of trends from
Incomes Data Services (IDS) reports showed that very few
piece-rate schemes had been installed since 1983; only 5
per cent of the newly introduced schemes reported by IDS
for manual workers were based on piecework. Moreover,
of the schemes mentioned by IDS as being abandoned,
piecework is the most frequent victim. However, the
information here is patchy, since it is invariably more
interesting to report the introduction of new schemes than
the demise of old ones.

The statistical evidence

Evidence from IDS reports is supported by statistics from

the Employment Department's New Earnings Survey. The NES statistics charted in Figures 1 and 2 show that although PBR schemes are still very widespread and the most important quantitatively, certainly for manual

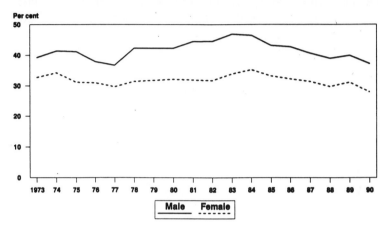

Figure 1 Proportion of manual employees who receive PBR, etc. Source. New Earnings Survey

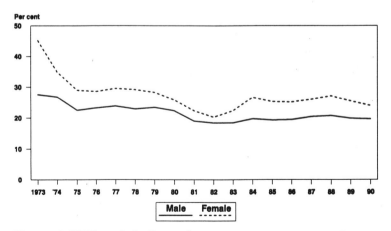

Figure 2 PBR and similar schemes as a percentage of earnings for manual employees who receive them. Source. New Earnings Survey

workers, they are in decline. Thus 37 per cent of all male manual workers received PBR payments in 1990, compared with 47 per cent in 1983. Similarly the proportion of female manual workers on piece-rate schemes peaked at 35 per cent in 1984, and by 1990 had fallen to 28 per cent. (The roughly comparable figures for 1951 were 28 per cent coverage among men and 41 per cent among women, which shows the growth in piecework which took place for men in the post-war period but also, in contrast, the decline in piecework for women.) Over the same period,

Table 1 PBR, etc., as a percentage of selected full-time male manual workers' average earnings[1] for those in receipt of incentive payments

Occupational category	1974	1984	1988	1989	1990
Material processing (excluding metals)	28·3	20·1	20·4	17·0	18·0
Chemicals, gas, etc., plant operators	16·0	8·5	10·8	9·5	10·9
Process, making, repairing and related (metal and electrical)	29·0	17·8	19·3	18·9	18·7
Painting, repetitive assembling, product inspecting, packaging and related	27·3	19·3	18·5	17·5	17·9
Inspectors and testers (metals and electrical)	24·7	13·4	11·3	12·1	13·5
Packers, bottlers, canners, fillers	25·8	19·6	16·3	14·8	17·0
HGV drivers (over three tons)	24·9	22·3	24·3	24·1	23·5
Fork-lift truck drivers/ operators	26·4	23·1	20·5	20·3	18·0
Storekeepers	20·3	16·0	15·2	14·9	14·4
General labourers	21·5	20·2	21·0	21·0	21·8
Bricklayers	29·8	28·1	26·7	26·7	28·8

[1] Less overtime pay.
Source. New Earnings Survey, Vol. D.

piece rate as a proportion of earnings for those manual workers covered by PBR schemes has not, however, varied greatly, as Figure 2 shows. For men the proportion averages around 20 per cent and for women the average fluctuates around 26 per cent.

Tables 1 and 2 show that in the main PBR, as a percentage of average earnings for those in receipt of it, has also remained fairly steady since the early to mid-1980s, after reaching a peak in 1974.

Table 2 PBR, etc., as a percentage of selected full-time female manual workers' average earnings[1] for those in receipt of incentive payments

Occupational category	1974	1984	1988	1989	1990
Material processing (excluding metals)	41·9	26·9	28·3	23·3	22·9
Making and repairing (excluding metals and electrical)	57·0	50·4	44·2	46·5	46·2
Painting, repetitive assembling, product inspecting, packaging and related	27·2	22·2	21·2	21·6	21·0
Packers, bottlers, canners, fillers	23·5	18·5	16·7	21·4	18·6
Sewing machinists (textiles)	66·9	60·1	55·3	52·7	53·5

[1] Less overtime pay.
Source. New Earnings Survey, Vol. D.

The results of the current survey support the conclusion that piece rate is by no means dead. One in five of all organizations responding to the survey were operating PBR for some of their manual employees, and 23 per cent of manufacturing companies were still operating piece-rate schemes (see Table 3). Of the organizations using piece rates, only 2 per cent (in the manufacturing sector) included all their manual employees. There was evidence

Table 3 Organizations that were operating individual PBR for manual employees (%)

	Priv.	Pub.	Manuf.	Serv.
All manuals	1	–	2	–
Some manuals	15	39	21	21
Base	274	79	171	187

Priv. Private sector. *Pub.* Public sector. *Manuf.* Manufacturing industries. *Serv.* Services.

that, where PBR schemes already existed, they frequently underwent revision to keep them 'fresh'. The survey showed that during the past five years 42 per cent of the piece-rate schemes still in existence had been substantially revised and 12 per cent had been extended to include other groups of manual employees.

Although piece-rate may not be dead, it is clearly in decline in the private manufacturing sector. The majority of the schemes covered by the survey had been introduced before the beginning of the 1980s, and indeed many if not most of them may well have been in place well before then. It was rare for new PBR schemes to be introduced. The survey found that just 3 per cent of the responding organizations had brought in new schemes in the past five years. Even more significantly, the survey revealed that 25 per cent of piece-rate schemes introduced before the mid-1980s had been withdrawn during the past five years.

The manufacturing sector

The shift from PBR was particularly marked in the manufacturing sector, and in discussions with personnel managers in such companies attention was focused on the reasons for the decline in piece-rate and what was replacing it. Most of the arguments are not new, and were probably put forward by opponents of PBR in the 1950s or even earlier. But others have emerged during the last decade or so, as a consequence of the greater attention now paid to quality and more flexible production. It appears that for some employers these new factors are tipping the balance away from piecework.

The 'old' arguments against piecework can be categorized as follows:

- *Lack of fairness and potential for industrial relations difficulties.* Earnings may fluctuate, sometimes through no fault of the individual (perhaps through lack of work or the need to learn a new job), leading to potential conflict. (Fluctuations are more marked in some sectors – for example, the clothing industry – than in others.)

  Work study values may be difficult to understand, are not necessarily accurate and are not always perceived as being fair. They do not create an environment of trust.
- *It does not necessarily work as an incentive.* Some operatives will decide how much money they want to make and, when they have produced enough to keep them happy, more or less pack up work for the week. There is no doubt that this is an old argument: see Alan Sillitoe's description of the Nottingham engineering industry in the 1950s in *Saturday Night and Sunday Morning!*

  Piecework can be manipulated. To quote one of the interviewees, 'there is scope for individuals to pull the wool over the eyes of the study officer: they find ways of beating the clock, if you like'.
- *It is costly to maintain.* Piecework requires a lot of work study and clerical personnel to maintain it. One company which abolished piece-rate reduced its work study and associated staff from twenty to one and a half. With piecework there is also a need for a separate quality control function.
- *It allows managers to escape their responsibilities.*

Instead of controlling production, costs and quality, some managers see the system as self-correcting and therefore not needing positive remedial action.

The additional arguments which carry more weight in present-day circumstances are:

- *It fails to encourage quality.* There is tension between the requirements of speed and quality. Under piecework workers may tend to do the job to the minimum acceptable standard, and there may be an incentive to ignore defects. Today's greater emphasis on quality, 'right first time' and 'continuous improvement' brings this issue into sharper focus. (It is worth noting that all the managers interviewed, including those staying with piecework, were aware of this tension.)
- *It discourages initiative.* As one interviewee said, 'people tend to get used to being told what to do'. Once upon a time this may not have mattered much; indeed, it may even have been seen as a positive advantage when the individual was regarded as an adjunct of the machine. Indeed, the only initiative it appears to encourage is that of 'beating the system'. In an era when all employees, and not just managers, are increasingly expected to contribute more widely, piece rates can inhibit initiative.
- *It can actually penalize skill and inhibit skills acquisition.* Take the example of two workers, one highly skilled, versatile and able to do a variety of jobs; the other able to perform perhaps only one or two jobs competently. The temptation is for the supervisor to allocate the more difficult jobs to the more highly skilled individual and leave the routine tasks to the person with lower skills. The result is that the lower-skilled person can maximize piece-rate earnings, while the more flexible worker may never be fully able to do so. Furthermore, if other operatives see this happening,

it is unlikely to encourage them to acquire new skills or to volunteer for more varied work.

- *Shorter runs increase the lack of fairness.* With the shorter production runs required in much of today's manufacturing, operatives may have less opportunity to maintain top speed on a particular job before being switched to another, again with consequences for earnings. This has emerged as a particular problem in the clothing industry, because of the need for short runs to meet the changing demands of fashion.
- *Changes in technology make it outmoded.* In some industries where automation has increased, output is predictable and depends much less on the efforts of the operative. In such cases individual incentives of the traditional kind become irrelevant.
- *It can cause health and safety problems.* There is growing evidence that, in the short-cycle and repetitive types of operation associated with piecework, operatives who perform a single operation during most of their working time are likely to be particularly susceptible to repetitive strain injuries (RSI). This was always seen as a potential problem, but RSI is now more widely recognized, and there is greater emphasis on health and safety. Moreover, occupational psychologists suggest that high stress levels are associated with production-line systems. Especially where the pressures of piece-rate are involved, absenteeism is likely to be increased.

It is not suggested that all these arguments apply in every situation where PBR is in force, only that they are producing a gradual but growing move away from piecework. However, many organizations still use piecework in the belief that it is an effective motivator. This, coupled with an understandable feeling of 'better the devil you know . . .', will mean that it will be a long time before piecework disappears entirely, if it ever does.

'What is replacing piecework?' was one of the questions

asked in the interviews. The personnel managers interviewed were all clear about one thing: that changes in payment systems need to be made in the context of wider changes in work organization (for examples of this see the case studies). As one of them said, 'If you take out a piecework system without changing the other things, you are doomed to failure. If you take it out and do nothing, then all you've done is left a vacuum.'

Sometimes such changes were prompted by the introduction of new technology, which made the previous payment system less relevant, or by changes in the market which had prompted the development of just-in-time manufacturing, allied with the need to reduce work in progress and moves towards Total Quality Management. On other occasions, the motivation was simply that piece-rate was perceived as outdated and inefficient for some of the reasons outlined above. Although in these latter examples the technology may have remained much the same, other very obvious changes were made, notably moves towards team working which were accompanied and reinforced by further measures such as improved training and a different role for supervisors.

Most of the changes had been made in unionized environments, and the unions had generally welcomed them (sometimes after initial resistance). In most of the companies which had taken out PBR, labour turnover and absenteeism had fallen and profitability had not suffered.

In terms of pay, there are two main options favoured by companies moving from individual PBR:

- *Move to flat-rate pay without bonuses.* Sometimes this is linked with the introduction of single status, with shopfloor workers being given staff terms and conditions (see Case Study 1). Pay may also be linked to skill levels, so operators are graded according to the skills they possess.
- *Introduce group bonuses – in effect, group PBR.* In the

clothing and footwear industries this seems to be a popular measure when team working is being introduced (see Case Study 2), partly perhaps because to some extent it retains a system which people understand and with which they are familiar. Typically the team rather than the individual is paid on a quota of completed products. Everyone is paid the same rate: the labour content of each operation is added up and divided between the members of the team. Because the average performance of a group of people will vary much less than that of an individual, take-home pay tends to vary less over time than it did under the previous piecework system, thus resolving to some degree the problem of fluctuating earnings identified earlier as a particular issue facing garment manufacturers. In addition, group payment is said to enhance the cohesiveness of teams.

The case studies which conclude this chapter illustrate both these broad alternatives. They also demonstrate the additional measures which managements have taken to reinforce the shift from individual PBR and the cultural changes which need to accompany it. These measures can be summarized as follows:

- *Changing management style.* This was summed up by an interviewee in a company whose distribution section had moved to a group bonus system. 'In the classical incentive scheme system it was said that the incentive scheme managed the men, so, in other words, management did not have to be quite so keen to make sure they turned up, because they wouldn't get their money.' But, he continued, under the group bonus scheme, 'Management have to be more on their toes because otherwise the men would start to complain. If they were not achieving results they would be coming back and complaining – "You don't unload or load your lorries quickly enough," "The turn-round time is too long," "There's no one available in the warehouse," and "You schedule our journeys incorrectly." So you've got to be an even better manager.

'Managers had in fact reported that the group incentive system had brought some of the drivers closer to management in terms of improving the efficiency of the operation. Their motivation might have been the pay packet, and management's motivation might have been efficiency, but it puts pressure on management to actually reduce the turn-round times, and so on, and to set up meetings with the workers to seek ways of making improvements.'

- *Improving supervision.* Like managers, supervisors were finding that their role was changing. Particularly where teams are encouraged to manage themselves, and control the flow of work between team members, the number of supervisors had fallen (in clothing companies, typically by around one-third). But those who remained were finding that they were becoming more like junior managers and planners than the progress chasers many of them had been previously. This meant that steps had to be taken to improve their level of competence by training and by introducing revised criteria for recruiting new supervisors. (The example in Case Study 1 of the engineering company which was reluctant to abandon piecework in one of its subsidiaries, because it believed that its existing supervisors were not capable of managing without it, demonstrates the increased importance of the role of supervisors when the break is being made with PBR.)

- *Increasing training for shopfloor workers.* It was not only managers and supervisors who were receiving training to equip them for operating in a non-PBR environment. These changes were frequently linked with the need to improve quality and do things 'right first time'. Training in problem-solving and communication techniques had been carried out for shopfloor workers in companies making the break with piecework.

- *Taking other measures.* Companies abandoning individual PBR had frequently taken other measures to reinforce the intended cultural change, although only one of the firms visited had gone so far as to introduce staff status for all employees. Typically more minor and symbolic measures had been taken. For example, a company introducing team working had redecorated the factory so that, among other things, 'the toilets were fit for human beings and not just workers', as the interviewee put it. Other employers had improved welfare facilities.

Local authorities

There was less evidence of piece rates' decline in the public sector and particularly in local authorities: the survey showed that 39 per cent of the public-sector organizations (mainly local authorities) had PBR and 41 per cent had MDW. The New Earnings Survey reveals that for those male local authority workers covered by PBR, such as roadsweepers and dustmen, the proportion of earnings accounted for by piece-rate is similar to those in manufacturing, at around 20 per cent.

The interviews suggested that, in some local authorities, bonuses had become so routinized that they were paid automatically almost regardless of performance. As one interviewee said, '. . . basically bonus has been automatically paid for years without anybody really questioning what management are getting for it'. This led to a number of serious problems, for example:

- In certain occupations, such as refuse collection, employees have learned how to manipulate the system.

- This itself has led to inequalities, as some groups (e.g. school meals workers, home helps) have been unable to manipulate their bonuses to the same extent, or are disadvantaged because it is difficult to measure their performance and hence to introduce bonus schemes.
- Sometimes quality suffers, and the monitoring of performance is a continual problem.
- Some local authorities were paying more for certain jobs than the market required.
- Bonus schemes are in some cases becoming a major disadvantage when local authorities come up against commercial competitors in competitive tendering exercises.

Most of these problems are, of course, similar to those mentioned above in the context of manufacturing. However, local authorities appeared to be tackling the problems not by abandoning individual PBR, like some companies, but by shifting from one type of PBR to another, in some cases group PBR. There appeared to be little innovative thinking in local authorities about making a break with piecework. The advent of competitive tendering is, however, beginning to force local authorities to rethink their position, because otherwise their operations will prove to be more expensive than those of external tenderers.

CASE STUDY 1. TAKING OUT BONUS SYSTEMS AND HARMONIZING TERMS AND CONDITIONS OF THE MANUAL WORK FORCE WITH THE STAFF

The company's aim is to be a low-cost producer with fewer but more highly paid people and what a senior manager called 'new-style' managers. Bonus systems are viewed as ineffective, because people tend to be satisfied when they have reached a target: 'this is what I've agreed with the boss'. This is contrasted with a situation where a manager says, 'Let's do our best,' which is likely to achieve more performance than a bonus system because 'nobody really knows what their best is'. As the interviewee perceived it, '. . . the main problem with PBR is that it leads to the work force pulling in an opposite direction to management. The objective of the work force – to fiddle the scheme – is directly opposed to that of management – to get them to work as hard as possible.'

A new-style manager would emphasize the importance of continuous improvement, always trying to do better and finding better methods. Pay would follow from performance, not lead it. The objective of the company would be to be a good payer but one with a reputation for training people and stretching them in order to develop their abilities. Management want to create a firm in which people move around, and do not get stuck in a rut, in order to achieve this objective.

Motivation is seen by the management as more than just paying people. 'People have to be involved, communicated to, and feel they have an influence in so far as they can in their bit of the patch, so they have to be given feedback on their contribution on the whole on a regular basis – and that's where the foreman comes in.'

In four out of five business units the company had taken out the bonus. Through a process of questioning, instigated by the central personnel department, managers realized that bonuses were not really acting as an incentive. For example, in two units the bonus did not vary from week to week and so, the management concluded, it could not be working as a motivator. In another, the work force produced the same amount each week, getting away as quickly as they could: a 'job-and-finish system'. In another unit, when the bonus did fluctuate to some extent, managers felt that there had been too much dilution of the times allowed – to make allowance for waiting time, rest times and 'loo time, combing hair time, interruption time' (as the personnel director believed). The effect of the

bonus scheme was not high output but low effort. The
work force, in management's judgement, knew more than
any supervisor about the scheme and how to wangle it. In
all four business units, when new equipment came in,
there would be extensive renegotiation of times.

In addition to taking the bonus out the management
subsequently harmonized the terms and conditions of the
manual work force with those of the staff and improved,
both by training and by recruitment, the quality of the
supervision. The elimination of bonus was part of a wider
approach to 'changing the company', so that internal
mobility and training were accorded far more significance
than previously. Included in this were changes in production planning and control and the structure of the
organization.

After some initial resistance the changes were reported
to have gone down 'very well' with the unions. The
resistance from the union took the form of wanting to be
paid 'up front'. Management wanted to achieve exactly the
opposite effect: inducing the work force to accept the
changes, and then rewarding the effects of the changes
with pay increases. The changes meant that the business
units are more profitable, profit margins have increased,
output per head has gone up, and the ratio of direct to
indirect labour has improved, as have quality and delivery
peformance. Absenteeism has fallen.

Nevertheless the mechanism by which these changes in
performance materialized was not attributed by management mainly to the pay systems; but rather to the way the
whole culture and management system changed. In particular the management is less distant from the work force
and is less paternalistic. 'There is more respect on both
sides. There is greater understanding of the different roles
people play in the organization. People are more interested in the future of the company, and managers listen
more to people's ideas.'

Management perceived that they could introduce

change more quickly. Labour turnover has fallen because, in the personnel director's words, 'we have a more contented work force'. In addition there were savings on administration. Two out of three of the redundancies among administrative staff in one plant which occurred at the time of the consolidation of the bonus were directly linked with this. The elimination of the bonus scheme was seen by management as having removed certain points of conflict, and raised to a new plane the debates that take place between management and unions, so '. . . they now discuss more important issues affecting the whole company, so they don't debate what time it takes to go to the loo, but rather "What's happening to our quality?" "Are we meeting delivery dates?" "What of the changes?" "What are the salesmen doing?"'

One initial problem which began to develop after the elimination of the bonus was that some concern was expressed by certain groups about differentials. Management reacted by introducing job evaluation. After this process, which involved the union representatives, the number of shop stewards was reduced by nearly 50 per cent in one plant because without the bonus, and after having dealt with the appeals (5 per cent in all) over the job evaluation scheme, there was less for them to do.

In one of the company's subsidiaries, however, the management preserved the bonus scheme because the general manager felt that his supervisors remained too old-style to ensure performance without it. He believed that the work force would slow down if it did not have the bonus, and the supervisors would be unable to stop this because they were too old to change. More competent supervisors who could ensure performance without a bonus scheme would have to be better trained, take on a managerial role rather than one of materials and progress chasing, and would have to align their sentiments and loyalty with management rather than with the work force. The current supervisors had all been promoted from the work force and were felt to be still very much part of it.

At the time of the interview management in this factory were in the process of redefining the supervisory role. When this task was completed they were planning to retire most of the existing supervisors early, in the belief that new supervisors would be more able to motivate the work force, set targets and make sure they were met.

CASE STUDY 2. MOVING FROM INDIVIDUAL PIECEWORK TO TEAM WORKING AND A GROUP BONUS

This company is in an industry with a long tradition of piecework – the schemes in use in the company were introduced in the late 1950s and covered all manual workers. Jobs have conventionally been split into three basic grades, each with a different price per minute. The ways of measuring jobs have been the only real modification in the past thirty years; the company has built up a computerized database of times, so values can be compiled synthetically from details of a task without having to time every new job. The only other change was that there had been an increase in the extent of flexibility, so people were trained to be able to adapt to different grades of work. The scheme has a safeguard in case of machine problems or lack of work; earnings cannot fall below three-quarters of normal pay.

Management believe that the scheme has served the company well. But there was always a problem of fluctuations in earnings and the tension between speed and quality. Workers are supposed to show the supervisor if there are any defects either in their work or in that of others before they pass it on, but they often do not because it would slow them down. There was also felt to be a potential industrial relations problem underlying piecework: the interviewee said, 'The values have to be perceived as fair, otherwise there is conflict. It does not create an environment of trust.' Sometimes this caused work stoppages, although management was never absolutely sure whether it was because of the routine, boring nature of much of the work, or whether it was actually engendered by the payment system.

Management had also become increasingly aware of the disparity between the way in which they treated manual workers and staff. For example, a manual worker with twenty years' service gets less holiday than his daughter who has just joined the firm as a typist. Also 'Staff get paid a guaranteed wage, so there is an apparent lack of trust in manual workers in paying them only upon achievement of results.'

Management identified three other problems with piecework. First, it does not encourage flexibility. As workers get into a rhythm on one job and earn high wages they are reluctant to be switched to a job or machine with which they are less familiar. Supervisors have to make deals with them to protect their earnings or simply leave them on the existing job. Second, piecework is thought not to encourage initiative, as 'people tend to get used to being told what to do. They end up needing to be told what to do.' Third, the system requires a lot of work-study personnel to be employed, and a separate quality control function to be maintained.

However, the system was felt by management to have ensured high production and to motivate people to work hard and fast. This had helped the firm to achieve productivity levels which were high enough to survive the increased competitive pressures from the Far East and Third World countries.

The company is now developing new concepts of production – in particular, it is aiming to make the time between ordering and delivery as brief as possible, and to gear production much more closely to retail customers' requirements. This is expected to give a competitive advantage over countries which have to ship their products over considerable distances. Additional motives were financial pressure to reduce working capital and the feeling that, despite its past usefulness, piecework had become 'archaic'.

To achieve the desired changes the firm is introducing a team-working system of production, based on small cells of four or five people who produce the whole product, from beginning to end. This demands more flexibility of labour but cuts down the time for producing one unit from weeks to about an hour. Although production time per unit has not been reduced, work in progress has been cut by the virtual elimination of the time lag between what were previously different operations in different units of the factory. The quality control function has been removed, as teams are responsible for maintaining quality. Their need for supervision has been reduced.

At the time of the interview, cells were being piloted in two parts of the factory and the payment system had been adjusted to meet the requirements of the new system. Prior to the formation of the cells the operators were trained in interpersonal skills, problem-solving techniques and waste elimination. Management felt that, as they were giving teams more autonomy, they should respond by giving them what the human resource manager called 'virtually a salary'. This was seen very much in symbolic terms: 'it shows trust'. Under the new group bonus scheme 90 per cent of the pay will be basic, with a 10 per cent variable element depending on the output of the cell. So far no problems have arisen because of different performance levels between team members, although management are aware that difficulties could arise if teams were formed from members with different levels of ability and performance.

Cost, quality, output and employees' attitudes are all improving under the new system, which is likely to be introduced into the rest of the factory. The trade unions have been supportive of the innovations, as they too agree that piecework was confrontational, and they welcome initiatives to keep their members' jobs in the face of intense overseas competition.

The verdict on individual payment by results

- PBR can work well as a motivator for some people, but it pays too much attention to money as a motivator, and ignores other motivational factors. In any event, schemes need constant monitoring and review if people are not to be allowed to 'beat the system'.
- In terms of culture, encouragement of co-operation, achievement of high standards of quality, and the extension and flexible use of skills, individual PBR schemes provide no advantage and can be harmful.

3

Group pay systems

Group pay schemes developed because performance often relates to the work of a team or to those in a large unit or company working together. They can be divided into three categories:

- *Group payment by results*, in which bonus pay is divided among members of a group or team either equally or in an agreed ratio.
- *Plant/enterprise-wide bonus schemes*, which differ from group PBR in that they are based on the achievement of productivity targets set for a whole plant, site or unit. The total bonus is divided among all production members or employees on the same basis rather than by ratio.
- *Profit sharing/share option schemes* based on organizational performance, employees receiving annual cash or share bonuses, including employee share options, based on the profit made in the previous accounting year.

Profit-sharing schemes reflect the overall performance of the total organization and differ fundamentally in type and generally in frequency from other types of bonus payments aimed at collective performance which concentrate more on groups of employees within the organization. The latter are essentially performance-related, aimed at encouraging closer links between pay and collective productivity rather than reflecting profitability.

Group payment by results

Twenty-three per cent of organizations in the survey used group PBR for some manual employees. Table 4 shows that the public sector most often uses group PBR for manual employees, 54 per cent of public-sector organizations using it, compared with 21 per cent of manufacturing companies. (Because of its nature, group PBR is unlikely to cover all employees, i.e. non-manual and manual, unless they are all employed in autonomous groups, each with its own bonus scheme.) Twelve per cent of organizations had 'group PBR' for some non-manuals – mostly managerial and professional grades (9 per cent), 5 per cent for senior management and 3 per cent for secretarial and clerical employees, but it is thought likely that these were group peformance-related pay schemes rather than 'non-manual group piece-rate'.

The number of respondents saying they were using group PBR in the survey was too small for any definite conclusions to be drawn about its increase or demise. Nor does the New Earnings Survey provide any clues, because it does not normally distinguish between types of incentive schemes. (In the 1977 New Earnings Survey more detailed questions were addressed to this issue. The responses to that enquiry showed that schemes based on individual performance were more widespread – in terms of number of employees covered – than schemes based on group performance, which in turn were more widespread than schemes based on company performance. A similar 'one-off' New Earnings Survey in the 1990s might produce interesting results, and would enable comparisons to be drawn with the situation in 1977.)

Almost certainly the largest exponent of group PBR is the industrial civil service, with over 70,000 employees covered. There is only one true piecework scheme remaining in the whole of the industrial civil service, and the trend is to move from measured daywork schemes to what

Table 4 Types of group incentive payment schemes in use for non-manual and manual employees (% of organizations)

Extent of use	Group PBR				Plant/enterprise bonus schemes				Profit-sharing/ share options		
	Priv.	Pub.	Manuf.	Serv.	Priv.	Pub.	Manuf.	Serv.	Priv.[1]	Manuf.	Serv.[2]
All employees	2	–	1	2	5	–	6	3	30	26	36
All non-manuals	–	–	–	–	1	–	2	1	4	4	4
Some non-manuals	15	1	12	13	6	4	6	4	20	24	15
All manuals	3	–	4	1	3	1	4	1	1	2	–
Some manuals	12	54	17	25	7	14	10	6	2	2	1
Base	274	79	171	187	274	79	171	187	274	171	108

Priv. Private sector. *Pub.* Public sector. *Manuf.* Manufacturing. *Serv.* Services.

[1] Twenty-three (6%) organizations employed no manual grades.
[2] Excluding public administration/health.

are known as efficiency schemes. (Under the former, the bonus is directly related to work standards while, under the latter, targets are set for overall productivity at the beginning of the year.) One reason for this trend is that there is now little genuine manufacturing work in the industrial civil service; most of the operations are in the nature of repair and maintenance – for example, ship repair – which do not readily lend themselves to piece working. Currently the split between MDW and efficiency schemes is about fifty-fifty.

If these targets are met, there is a £35 weekly bonus; if they are not met, an adjustment is made on the next year's payment. In short, there has been a change in the approach to monitoring the way people work, which involves (for example) line managers constantly measuring activity and random activity sampling rather than the whole gamut of work study. The changes have been accompanied by agreements with the unions to increase flexibility, reduce demarcations, and have bell-to-bell working, so that the resultant real increases in pay have been self-financing.

In the interviews one example was found of a company moving from (mainly) group PBR to time-based payments.

CASE STUDY 3: ABANDONING GROUP PBR AS A RESULT OF CHANGING MANAGEMENT PHILOSOPHY AND INTRODUCING NEW TECHNOLOGY

In a foundry, at normal working with even rhythm, quality is not thought to be adversely affected by the use of piecework. There can, though, be a trade-off between quality and quantity when high output is required and the operators push too hard. Management in the company have long believed that at both low and at very high levels of production quality deteriorates.

In the past all the work of a foundry required very high levels of physical exertion. Some form of PBR existed in all the firm's twenty-eight plants: some schemes were time saved/standard hours-based, while others were straight piecework. A typical scheme still in operation is a group bonus system built around an estimate of the performance of the moulding machines. If the machines are capable of producing an average of 160 boxes an hour, for example, then the bonus is geared so that a basic wage can be paid for, say, 150 boxes, and then a very steep bonus curve is set to 'incentivize' production from this figure to a peak production level. Although the men cannot directly influence the cycle of the moulding machines, what they can influence is the down time.

The bonus system is thus aimed at motivating them to get machines mended as soon as possible when they break down, by making sure that maintenance men attend to them immediately, as well as operators helping whenever possible with the repairs. The philosophy underlying the scheme is that, unless the bonus curve is steep, both the fitters and operators have an interest in down time, as neither have an incentive to get machines working quickly after a breakdown.

When products are changed the pattern is changed, and it is possible to lose as many as fifteen or sixteen boxes in the work cycle change-over. However, the 'clever guy' (as the personnel director called him) can make a change-over in the cycle and may not even drop a box. Whilst there are differences in the basic pay of members of the work team, all get the same bonus under the above scheme. The variation in week-by-week bonus is typically about 5 per cent. Effort is usually pretty stable, and down time is the major cause of variation.

Owing to changes in technology, work in some plants has become more machine-paced and now requires less physical effort. There has also been a move from piecework to time-based payments, reflecting the technological change, but also driven by the need to cope with variability in the product mix.

The firm has now reached a new stage of technological

development. Its latest investment has been a complete overhaul of an existing plant with the latest technology and equipment in order to produce a completely new range of products, with a considerably increased level of automation. Piecework has been abandoned here, and all the operators are paid a fixed rate on a monthly basis. Although the factory reflects a leap in technology, the move to the new payment system reflects a change in managerial philosophy. The personnel director put it thus: 'It is a recognition that output's fine, but if you want to be a Total Quality business, and you want people with high-quality skills, and you want to motivate people, then there are things about incentives which give you unfortunate people effects like resistance to change and an undue emphasis on output at the expense of quality and innovation.'

The new pay system is seen by management as a response to a new question: 'How can we use the people better?' and as such contrasts with the previous system, which was better fitted to responding to an outdated question: 'How can we make people sweat more?' In the plant in which piecework has been abandoned a number of grades based on a number of skill modules have been introduced, each operator being given an opportunity to acquire each skill level. The only incentive in the system is to rise up the grading system.

Training is seen as the main method by which the TQM philosophy will be achieved. The aim is to inculcate a 'right first time' attitude. All operators are trained in interpersonal skills, job instruction skills, problem-solving and preventive methods, and how to do skills profiles. There is a room with a flip chart to which they are encouraged to go when problems arise to think and brainstorm them through.

The two most significant changes from the conventional plant are therefore in the payment system and employment package and in the vastly increased training given to the workers. The new factory is seen as an experiment, and the intention is to extend the harmonization and new practices to all factories, including the abandonment of PBR if they are deemed successful. Management believe that they will be able to motivate without piecework and are monitoring the plant's output, quality and absenteeism rates in particular for proof of this. Piecework fitted a culture in which output was the main priority, possibly at the expense of quality, stockholding costs and return on capital employed. The new aim, in the words of the interviewee, is 'to make everybody a thinker, so they are asking, "Is the quality right?"'. The foundry needs to inculcate a willingness to stop and investigate what's going wrong, something which would not happen under piecework, where people would carry on producing while knowing that the items being produced were defective.

Plant or enterprise-wide bonus schemes

Plant or enterprise-wide bonus schemes were operated by just 12 per cent of organizations participating in the survey, but in only 4 per cent of organizations were all employees included. As might be expected, process and craft workers were twice as likely to receive such bonuses in the manufacturing sector (17 per cent of companies) as in the service sector (7 per cent). Nine per cent of manufacturing companies had some secretarial and clerical grades covered by such schemes, and 4 per cent in the service sector. In the public sector 15 per cent of organizations operated enterprise-wide bonus schemes for manual employees but only 1 per cent for secretarial and clerical grades. There was no significant difference between the private and public sectors in the extent to which these bonus schemes were used for manual grades, but non-manuals were more likely to be included in the private-sector industries (see Tables 4 and 5).

Table 5 Types of group incentive payment schemes in use, by category of employee (% of organizations)

Category	Group PBR				Plant/enterprise bonus schemes				Profit-sharing/ share options		
	Priv.	Pub.	Manuf.	Serv.	Priv.	Pub.	Manuf.	Serv.	Priv.	Manuf.	Serv.[1]
Directors/senior executives	6	–	4	6	6	3	7	4	55	56	54
Management/professionals	10	1	6	11	7	3	9	4	45	42	52
Secretarial/clerical administrative	4	–	4	3	8	1	9	4	36	32	43
Process/craft ancillary	14	54	19	26	12	13	17	7	27	26	26
Base	274	79	171	187	274	79	171	187	274	171	108

Priv. Private sector. *Pub.* Public sector. *Manuf.* Manufacturing. *Serv.* Services.

[1] Excluding public administration/health.

Profit-sharing and share option schemes

In parallel with the drive for closer links between individual pay and performance in recent years, in the private sector considerable attention has also focused on strengthening the link between pay and profitability. There has therefore been a growth in profit-related pay, the most common types being profit-sharing and employee share option schemes. Such schemes have been boosted by favourable tax arrangements introduced by various Finance Acts over the past decade. Among the aims are to encourage employers to use such schemes to increase employees' identification with the company; to enable them to share in its success; to stimulate greater interest in its profits and financial results; and to encourage employees to feel that their own efforts, individually and collectively, can contribute to success. Such schemes are based on organizational performance, employees receiving annual cash or share bonuses, including employee share options, based on the profit made in the previous accounting year.

Of all group performance-related pay schemes, it is clear that profit-sharing schemes are the most popular: 55 per cent of the private-sector companies in the survey had such schemes. The survey confirmed that, compared with the previous decade, the 1980s saw rapid growth in the introduction of profit-sharing for non-manual grades. Prior to the 1980s 16 per cent of the companies in the survey had profit-sharing schemes; during the 1980s a further 34 per cent introduced them, most during the past five years. As Figure 3(a) shows, during this same period more than a third of those schemes already in existence had been revised, some had been extended to other non-manual groups (presumably non-management) but only three schemes had been withdrawn. Although the coverage of profit-sharing schemes is not as extensive as performance-related pay among non-manual employees,

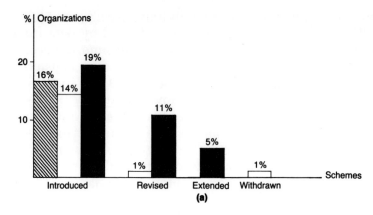

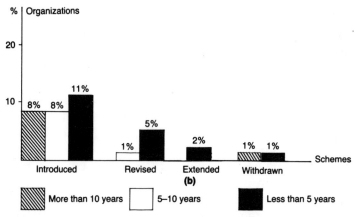

Figure 3. The growth of profit-sharing and share option schemes for (a) non-manual and (b) manual employees. N = 274

the rate of introduction since the mid-1980s has been similar.

Although the growth of profit-sharing for manual employees was slower, there was nevertheless steady expansion, with 19 per cent of companies extending their schemes to manual grades during the past decade. Some of the earlier schemes covering manuals were substantially revised, but just three were withdrawn (see Figure 3(b)).

The results of the survey are confirmed by data from other sources. According to the Inland Revenue, in December 1991 581,000 employees were covered by registered profit-related pay schemes, a rise of 313,600 in twelve months. A Department of Employment survey (Hibbett, 1991) has shown that employee share schemes and group incentive and bonus payments have risen substantially – from 53·2 per cent in 1988 to 76·9 per cent of all companies in 1991. Over half of all the department's survey companies had a share scheme which all employees could join.

Whilst the present survey showed that profit-related pay was still more likely to be available to senior management (55 per cent of firms) and other management and professional grades (45 per cent), there were distinct signs of it being extended to non-management grades: secretarial and clerical employees were covered in 36 per cent of companies, and process, craft and ancillary workers in 27 per cent. One-third of companies operated profit-sharing schemes for all their employees, although not all these organizations employed manual grades.

Profit-sharing and share option schemes covered non-manual grades in the service sector more frequently than in manufacturing; 52 per cent of the service organizations involved 'other management levels and professionals' (i.e. below senior executive) and 43 per cent other non-management non-manuals, compared with 42 per cent and 32 per cent respectively in the manufacturing organizations (see Tables 4 and 5). Profit-sharing and share option schemes for all grades of employee were most likely to exist in large companies with over 5,000 employees. However, such schemes were by no means the prerogative of large organizations and, as Table 6 shows, they were popular among companies in all size bands.

Despite profit-sharing's popularity, the personnel managers interviewed (with to some extent one exception – see

Table 6 Profit-sharing/share option schemes by size of company (private sector only) and category of employee (% of companies)

	Number of employees						
	250 or less	251–500	501–1,000	1,001–5,000	5,001–10,000	10,001–25,000	Over 25,000
Directors/senior executives	47	59	53	52	50	59	84
Management/professionals	44	50	42	39	55	53	63
Secretarial/clerical administrative	35	41	31	29	46	59	59
Process/craft ancillary	16	28	19	21	46	53	33
Base	32	44	52	89	20	15	22

Case Study 4 at the end of this chapter) did not regard it as an incentive because it does not relate to individual performance (people cannot see how their performance has an impact on corporate performance) and because the amounts of money involved are too small. As one manager put it, 'I don't see profit-sharing as an incentive. I can't actually get more pay by improving my performance – it's not geared to what I have control over and making sure I get paid for what I do.' In some cases this was because profit-sharing had not paid out significant sums, in others because it was seen as 'something that just happens at the end of the year: not a real motivator'. The following view was fairly typical: 'I don't think profit share has done anything, because the amount is too small and it is on a group basis. I don't for one minute think that people buckle to and think, "I must work extremely hard to improve my profit performance."'

Some managers explicitly referred to profit-sharing as a reward system, in contrast to an incentive system. For example, in one manufacturing firm the interviewee saw profit-sharing as simply 'giving people a slug of the action at the end of the year. I don't think it incentivizes people particularly; it does not make them concentrate on things that matter.'

One firm with a share ownership scheme had tackled this question head-on by amending the scheme to aid retention and to operate as a reward. To help retention, instead of being given large blocks of shares every four years, employees were given smaller tranches annually, so that at any point in time they had some options they could not realize. Second, in order for share options to operate as a reward, management switched from setting the amount awarded according to salary level to deciding it on the basis of personal performance.

Other interviewees saw at least two advantages in profit-sharing. The first was that profit-sharing based on a fixed proportion of salary was thought to be fair. One said,

'The company had a good year financially and there is a couple of per cent increase, which is not very much, but in terms of a lump sum payment it can be a few hundred pounds. That can be very welcome, and it comes out in time for the holidays.'

The second perceived merit was that it highlighted the importance of company performance, although often this came out in a rather negative context. For example, in a company which had made no profit the previous financial year the interviewee said, 'It increases understanding that if you don't make profit you can't pay: in that sense it focuses attention, but it is not a motivator per se.' Another interviewee said, 'Profit-sharing may be more of an incentive than you'd think. Put it this way. When it's there it's taken for granted. But we've had a year when it wasn't there, and that caused a major outcry – people saying, why was there not to be a profit share? I believe that having it and reviewing it focuses people on how the business is doing.'

But in some cases there were profit shares which 'people did not think about,' as one respondent put it, because they had not generally paid out in the past decade. Remoteness, too, could be a problem: those covered by corporate profit-sharing schemes could be in units which might be doing well or might be doing badly but, because the annual pay-out related to the performance of the company as a whole, it did not reflect their part of the business. One company visited was tackling this by breaking the profit-sharing system down so that it no longer related to the whole group, but to each subsidiary. The idea '. . . was to bring it closer to home and that the schemes should be related to the company which the individual could influence the results of and feel a part of'.

For one firm, as Case Study 4 shows, profit-sharing was nevertheless the central plank of its pay policy.

This company introduced profit-sharing for all its employees in 1980. Eligibility was initially based on two years' service. This was reduced to one year's service in 1990, although those with only one year's service get only 50 per cent of the profit-share. The profit-share, which tends to be around 10 per cent of pay, can be taken in cash, in shares or in a mixture of both. The profit-share is not usually linked to performance, though very occasionally for especially good performance people can get one and a half times their salary. It is viewed by management as a long-term retainer, and an incentive for the company to do well and for executives to reap some reward for that profit. For senior managers there is also a share option scheme, whereby they receive, for example, the equivalent of their annual salary in shares.

The general philosophy on remuneration is that the company is 'not seeking to be the best in terms of pay, holidays, sick-pay schemes, clothing allowances or the minor benefits. We know some of our competitors are better – for example, in terms of holidays. Where we are the best is that we want people to enjoy the success of our business and want to increase our employees' shareholding in the business. The advantage to the company is that employees are perceived to be genuinely interested in the share price. The most tangible benefit is seen to be that it helps to retain staff. It's a part of the company's culture that we want to promote; we are proud that we have one of the best profit-sharing schemes in the country.'

The profit-sharing scheme was reported as having practical effects on morale, but was seen less as a motivator than as a retainer: the firm averages 30–40 per cent labour turnover, and the aim is to reduce turnover to as low a figure as possible because it is very costly to train people. However, the company does not believe that it is possible to estimate the scheme's impact on labour turnover. 'Other factors intervene, like the recession; it's always a question of what would our turnover be if we had not done this, it could have been far worse – that's always the difficulty.'

The verdict on group pay systems

- Group PBR and even plant and enterprise-wide bonus schemes share with individual PBR the need for continual revision if they are not to fall into 'disrepair'. Revisions of such schemes may increasingly have to focus on the need to encourage the improvement of skills, co-operation and flexibility.
- Profit-sharing schemes are not seen to work as incentives because they contain no individual performance element and the money involved is generally small. However, to some extent they can focus attention on corporate performance and help to retain employees. In theory at least, profit-sharing should provide a basis for participation in organizational success without commitment to maintaining payments during a downturn.

4

The rise of individual performance-related pay

Broader and deeper

The impression that individual performance-related pay (PRP) is tending to replace many of the fixed incremental systems which existed previously was confirmed by the present survey and by the review of settlements from 1983. Both of these showed that it has spread from senior management to non-manuals generally. There is also evidence that in some cases PRP is now moving downwards to cover manual grades as well.

The survey shows that PRP is not strictly a 1980s phenomenon: 32 per cent of the PRP schemes for non-manual grades currently in operation had been introduced over ten years ago. But 40 per cent of PRP schemes for non-manuals had been introduced within the last ten years – 27 per cent during the past five years, see Figure 4(a), so PRP is spreading broader and deeper. There is virtually no evidence of PRP schemes being withdrawn, although the survey discovered that, like all payment schemes, they are reviewed and substantially revised from time to time.

Almost half the private-sector companies (47 per cent) in the survey had PRP schemes for all non-manual grades (i.e. including other staff than managers), and a further 21 per cent were also using PRP for some non-manuals (see Table 7). There was no significant difference between manufacturing and service industries, but there was a difference between the public and private sectors. In the public sector 37 per cent of organizations in the survey were operating PRP schemes for some of their non-manual grades, but only 6 per cent covered all non-manuals. Non-management grades in the public sector were signifi-

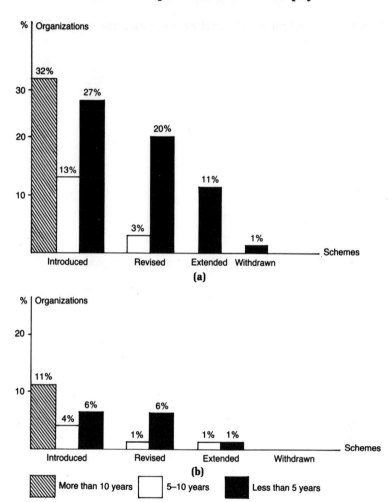

Figure 4. The growth of performance-related pay schemes for (a) non-manual and (b) manual employees. N = 360

cantly less likely to be covered by PRP than in the private sector, and those employed in senior management, management and professional occupations were nearly twice as likely to be eligible for PRP in the private sector as those

Table 7 Coverage of performance-related pay (% of organizations)

Extent of coverage	Private	Public	Manufacturing	Services
All em- ployees[1]	28	3	13	30
All non- manuals	19	3	25	6
Some non- manuals	21	37	22	27
All manuals	2	1	2	2
Some manuals	7	8	6	7
Base	274	79	171	187

[1] Twenty-three organizations (6%) had no manual employees.

Table 8 Performance-related pay by category of employee and sector (% of organizations)

Category	Private	Public	Manufacturing	Services
Directors/ senior executives	58	28	53	50
Management/ profes- sionals	66	34	59	58
Secretarial/ clerical ad- ministrative	56	10	46	44
Process/craft ancillary	24	9	18	23
Base	274	79	171	187

in the public sector (see Table 8). In the private sector 56 per cent of companies in the survey had some secretarial and clerical grades on PRP.

This contrasted with the situation in the public sector,

where only 10 per cent of the respondents had some secretarial and clerical grades covered by PRP. However, the situation is changing rapidly: in 1991 the government announced that, as part of its Citizen's Charter initiative, PRP was to be extended further. There should, it said, be a 'regular and direct link between remuneration and standards of service'. HMSO (one of the new 'Agency' departments) and the Royal Mail are two large public-sector organizations which introduced performance pay for substantial numbers of staff during 1991, and as this book goes to press the government was renegotiating with the main civil service unions the long-term agreements governing the pay of the majority of civil servants, with the aim of introducing comprehensive performance pay systems. Elsewhere in the public sector the pay review bodies for teachers and nurses indicated their intentions of developing PRP for those groups.

The spread of PRP in the public sector has been reported in a number of other recent studies. A Local Authorities' Conditions of Service Advisory Board (LACSAB) survey (PRP Report No. 4, 1990) revealed that 39 per cent of local authorities had performance-related pay schemes in force or had taken a definite decision to introduce them, while a further 27 per cent were considering them. LACSAB also noted that, whilst they were usually applied to senior employees, 25 per cent of authorities had extended what they described as merit schemes to all grades of non-manual staff and that there was a widespread intention to extend the schemes down through the organizational hierarchy. A study in two local labour markets – Leicester and Reading – by the Policy Studies Institute in Spring 1990 for the Department of Employment found 36 per cent of public-sector organizations with some form of PRP (Casey et al., 1991).

The present survey also indicated that PRP is penetrating down to manual workers. Long (1986) suggested that at the time of her research 24 per cent of organizations

surveyed had extended their performance review systems
to skilled manual grades, but there was no evidence that
PRP was also being applied to manual workers. According
to our own survey, 21 per cent of organizations (24 per cent
of private-sector companies) had PRP for at least some of
their process and craft grades. Six per cent of respondents
had introduced PRP for manual workers in the period
1986–91, with a further 5 per cent revising existing
schemes – see Figure 4(b). The review of settlements
identified fifteen companies which had introduced PRP
for manual workers between 1983 and 1991 (the comparable figure for non-manuals was sixty-six firms).

What is not clear is the proportion of manual workers
covered by PRP in the survey companies; it might be
relatively small, but PRP for manuals as well as non-
manuals seems to be a growing trend. The PSI study
mentioned above found that over a third of organizations
employing craft operatives and plant or machine operators
had some form of appraisal-based PRP for these grades.

The trend towards PRP is not, however, reflected in the
official statistics. Its growth should be shown in the 'PBR,
etc., payments' component of the New Earnings Survey,*
but it is not. According to the NES, such payments have
been fairly steady for non-manual workers for the last few
years at around 15 per cent of earnings, while for manuals
any growth in PRP is disguised simply as piece-rate
earnings. The reason may be that it is very difficult in some

---

* This is defined as 'The sum, within an employee's gross
earnings, of all payments, for the pay-period, under piecework
and other payment-by-results systems, bonuses including profit-sharing, commission and other incentive payments with the
possible exception of any relating to overtime hours and treated
as overtime earnings. Where such payments are made in each
pay-period it includes the amount paid in the survey pay-
period; where they are made less frequently, the proportionate
amount for one pay-period, based on the last payment or the next
payment if known, is included.'

Table 9 Performance-related pay by size of organization and category of employee (% of companies)

Category	Number of employees						
	250 or less	251–500	501–1,000	1,001–5,000	5,001–10,000	10,001–25,000	Over 25,000
Directors/senior executives	41	49	53	66	42	45	45
Management/professionals	43	53	64	85	58	52	64
Secretarial/clerical administrative	35	38	54	55	46	27	45
Process/craft ancillary	14	23	17	18	38	18	30
Base	37	53	59	106	26	44	33

cases for wages and salaries staff completing NES enquiry forms to apportion the gross payments received by employees: for example, should accelerated increment schemes and ones with an efficiency bar be categorized as incremental schemes or 'PBR, etc., payments'? Schemes in which salaries for members of a group are all individually determined, and do not even have a formal cost-of-living adjustment or general increase component, are also difficult to categorize in the headings laid down by the NES.

Although the NES figures do not reflect the changes which have taken place, the evidence from the present survey is confirmed by ACAS, which found in 1988 (Occasional Paper 45, 1990) that a quarter of firms contacted had introduced some form of PRP in the previous three years and another fifth were considering its introduction or further extension. Similarly, in 1988 the CBI found that 57 per cent of companies participating in its Pay Databank linked at least some of the employees' pay to both company and individual performance; 28 per cent used only individual performance, and the most popular type of scheme was 'variable merit pay'.

Why has PRP grown?

The rest of this chapter looks at the various reasons for the growth of PRP given by the personnel managers who were interviewed. A mixture of motives was found. The reasons can be categorized under the following headings, although clearly there is substantial overlap between them:

- Problems with incremental systems.
- Reward and motivation.
- Promotion of cultural and organizational change.
- Improving communication.
- Improving recruitment and retention.
- Individualizing employee relations.

There were particular differences of view about whether their organizations' main aim in introducing PRP had been to reward or to motivate: in this respect, there is a contrast with traditional PBR, which can be regarded purely as a motivator (although its effectiveness as such is debatable).

Problems with incremental systems

The adoption of PRP meant in the case of non-manuals abandoning incremental pay scales, which were seen as giving little or no flexibility, particularly to reward those who were perceived to be doing well. As one respondent put it, '. . . not enough recognition is given to differences in performance'. This is certainly a motive in the civil service: as another interviewee said, 'The biggest criticism of the civil service-type incremental system is that it gives no incentive to the person who has hit the ceiling.' One respondent described the pre-PRP regime thus: 'We had a wide pay range and people progressed to the top of it. Pay was reviewed each year, but there was an inevitability about increases, and you then stuck at the top. You got a share option, company car, etc., and it was all very assured.'

Incremental systems were in some cases explicitly associated with unmotivated performance. In an insurance company which had attempted to alter its approach radically by abandoning incremental pay scales and many of its generous fringe benefits, including mortgage benefit, in favour of PRP the interviewee said, 'I as a personnel manager saw a number of cases where you have a fairly difficult problem surrounding a senior or middle manager who is unmotivated, who is on the gravy train, and who is not doing his job properly and is very difficult to get rid of. Extraordinarily difficult to get rid of under the old insurance ethos.'

Other organizations seemed to be less concerned about unmotivated employees – several felt that most of their

employees were good performers – but were more concerned about retention and recruitment. The incremental
scales meant, in many cases, that particular people's
salaries were not in line with market rates. Another
interviewee assessed the impact of PRP like this: 'Recruitment and retention have been much easier. Younger
managers are much more confident that they will not have
to put in their twenty-five years before they reach a salary
level which rewards their experience and performance.'

Rather than abandoning its incremental system, one
firm had adjusted it to allow for people who were
consistently performing well. The aim was to continue to
get the good performers to the top of the range as fast as
they could go, but also to give managers the ability to
reward the top performer consistently better than the good
performer, in this case 10 per cent higher. Rather than
moving over to fully fledged performance pay, it was
envisaged that the appraisal system would be sharpened
up, so that the high performers could be identified:
'marking the difference' was the phrase used within the
company. The interviewee justified the firm's attitude
thus: 'We have always believed you don't win by turning
things on their head. We mustn't overturn the incremental
system, just refocus it. We've got an appraisal system
which we mustn't throw out. Through the appraisal
mechanism, performance will be assessed on a more
objective basis. It will be down to the manager's discretion
to set pay.'

In summary, automatic increases under incremental
schemes were generally seen as lacking fairness, giving no
incentive and meaning that in some cases salaries could be
out of line with market rates, giving rise to difficulties of
recruitment and retention. PRP was being introduced to
remedy these perceived difficulties.

Reward and motivation

It was clear that rewarding the better performers at the expense of the poorer ones was central to many of the recently introduced PRP schemes. The key thing, for many interviewees, was the relativities: 'not to reduce everybody to the lowest common denominator', as one put it. Or, as another said, 'If people give exceptional performance they should get exceptional pay.' Rewarding initiative was also an important factor, as an interviewee from a financial organization said: 'With a small number of relatively senior people at our head office, we want people who have individual initiative. We don't have hordes of people doing the same thing but want people to be involved and to exercise their initiative. Therefore we want to pay them on a system which demonstrates that we recognize initiative.'

Schemes had also been introduced to motivate people, although not only through money: PRP linked with appraisal was seen as also motivating, through giving recognition, feedback and clear direction. The general impression, however, was that, although motivation was certainly a factor in the introduction of schemes, it was less significant than rewarding good performance. Certainly, interviewees were by no means certain that PRP did succeed in motivating, and this issue is discussed more fully in the next chapter.

Promotion of cultural and organizational change

For many interviewees PRP had been introduced with the primary objective of helping to change the organizational culture. One personnel manager in a manufacturing firm clearly saw it in these terms: 'Introducing PRP was a key event, really. It was a break with the past which said, "You'll always get an increase every year, you'll always get a minimum increase, and on top of that you'll get something else, and it doesn't matter how you perform." Now what we're saying is, "Nobody owes anybody a thing. Nobody gets a pay rise unless they earn a pay rise," so it is a total break.' He and other managers in similar situations particularly saw the break as being towards a 'very commercial organization which is more focused, in which we want everybody to contribute and are saying they will prosper and share in the wealth if they contribute.'

Another example was the public-sector organization which now received its money indirectly (i.e. through the work it did for other public agencies and not directly from central government as before), but which was being encouraged to diversify. 'We had to become more a customer- and cost-oriented organization, though still a public body, one in which profit was no longer a dirty word. We are expected to operate as if we were in the private sector – out there in the real world with competitors. In the past the customer was someone you told what he wanted and when he could expect to get it and what it was going to cost him. Now the customer comes first and we have to make sure our work is cost-effective.'

In local authorities the changes imposed by central government, including competitive tendering and local management of schools, meant that 'councils have needed to show that they are as lean and efficient as possible'. In local government and other public agencies, as elsewhere, the move to PRP was part of a more general attempt to introduce objectives-based management, and greater accountability on the part of managers. As one personnel officer of a local authority put it, 'The general theory is that you focus on the objectives of the organization and means of achieving them and have a mechanism for rewarding good performers.' Here each manager's job was first evaluated, the principal accountabilities were identified, and finally actual targets and objectives were set. As another local authority interviewee said, 'Under compulsory competitive tendering we have now to compete with the private sector. What has come from this is that we have to adopt a business culture. We have had to use incentive schemes for commercial purposes, that is, to get value for money, to consider motivation as part of the overall objectives of running that particular business.' Similarly, in the National Health Service, 'To some extent it [PRP] links in with the general desire to get the Health Service run on much more businesslike lines and a desire to link in the individual's objectives with the organization's objectives.'

One private-sector manager stressed that, when his firm had introduced PRP for its senior executives, 'The purpose was not to provide more money for senior executives but to get them to focus on things which mattered to the business. It was a way of crystallizing managers' minds on what are seen by the managing director to be the key targets.' In another firm, it was said, 'The company wanted to emphasize that individual managers are accountable for certain aspects of the business. We wanted to get away from consensus management and to get managers' income more geared to their profitability.'

A typical example of a firm which introduced PRP to increase accountability and to encourage a focus on key objectives was a manufacturer in the electronics industry.

CASE STUDY 5. THE CONTRACT WITH CAESAR

PRP had been introduced on the assumption that it had become the norm in the market place. Not, however, for recruitment and retention purposes, but because it was felt that if the company were paying market rates, and there were a variable element in pay, it might be able to get more out of the management team for the same salary bill. Two other reasons underlaid the introduction of PRP. First, the view that it would influence managers to channel effort into what the business wanted. Second, it was also seen as reinforcing a major new organization-wide initiative which was called the 'centurion concept'. This term was used, first, because the firm was approaching its one-hundredth year and, secondly, because the centurion had a contract with Caesar which he had to fulfil. In this company's case, managers would be set targets and must understand that they had to achieve them. PRP was seen as reinforcing this 'centurion' concept, and it offered a positive balance – 'If you succeed you'll be paid more' – to its negative side – 'If you don't deliver, you're out.' The centurion concept was seen as symbolic of the notion of a personnel contract by which each manager committed himself or herself to a set of targets which he or she would deliver.

* * *

In some cases PRP was linked with major reorganization and decentralization of decision-making. One such case was an insurance company which had fragmented itself, with business units built around certain product lines so that it could address differently the various markets it was in. As the interviewee said of the introduction of PRP, 'It was to get the business unit concept properly off the ground. Supervision of each business unit's managers now resides with the managing director. He has the final say over whether somebody gets a pay rise, or bonus, or share option. The head of each business unit is thus empowered to manage his managers far more than if the company had retained the old remuneration system.' Allied to this was what was seen as a move from a rather paternalistic style of organization, so that the company was 'now much less tolerant of passengers than it used to be in the past'.

The value of objective-setting in the context of cultural change is illustrated by the case of a company which had for long had a form of merit pay and, as part of an overall human resources development strategy aimed at promoting flexibility through harmonization, had introduced PRP for all employees.

CASE STUDY 6: MAJOR CULTURAL CHANGE – PRP FOR ALL

All salaried staff of the firm had been evaluated at the end of each year according to four categories: 'outstanding', 'commendable', 'standard' and 'unsatisfactory/unacceptable'. In 1990 the firm decided to revise the scheme. Previously people were not being set objectives. There was, in the words of the current compensation manager, 'poor definition of what people were supposed to be doing and a lack of clarity about the payment process which we had to make more specific'.

Senior management were not convinced that there was consistency throughout the company. An analysis of the distribution of rankings revealed that it was heavily skewed in favour of the 'commendable' gradation. The rationale for the revision was that management felt they 'wanted more value for money from pay and more consistency in the application of merit levels across the company throughout the UK'. Management decided to introduce objectives for all staff, as well as add a new fifth band in the appraisal system, so a category termed 'fair' was introduced between 'standard' and 'unsatisfactory'. Managers were '. . . retrained and re-educated in objective setting and appraisal'.

The expectation was that the introduction of the new scheme would mean a switch 'from an autocratic to a joint solving approach'. This was seen as a 'major cultural change', with a desire on the part of senior management to become more open in their management style. The perceived advantages of the objective-based PRP system over the previous merit pay are now seen to be that both the subordinate and his/her manager are involved in assessing the individual's performance; that the individual feels he or she has more influence on the outcome of the assessment on which his/her pay is based; and that it is viewed as much fairer and more sophisticated. Above all else, it is seen as serving what the compensation manager called 'a

need for feedback', since, as he put it, 'To operate in a
vacuum is more frustrating than having someone saying,
"You're doing a bad job."' Production workers, now called
'industrial staff', are also covered by performance appraisal, although the process for them differs from that of
managers, as the management wish 'to focus on slightly
different aspects in the two cases'.

The respondent offered the following examples. 'If you
look at a lab job, you might want to talk in terms of the
objectives a person should achieve in a year. They would
be one-off objectives, and their performance would be
monitored against them, ultimately at the performance
appraisal process, but also during the year. In the case of
industrial staff you are looking at more performance
standards. It is unlikely you would set an industrial staff
member a project to do, as a specific objective. It would be
the relationship he has with individuals, what's the
quality of work, is it completed according to schedule?'

The main rationale behind harmonization was
increased flexibility, 'versatility, broadening the work that
people are doing, their taking on board additional training,
their having performance appraisal. We were looking for
changes in work practices by the industrial staff in terms of
how jobs might change and develop.' Bringing in performance appraisal, as well as a new salary structure, was seen
as part of the whole exercise of converting people from
what were called manual workers to industrial staff, and
the aim was 'to try to engender perhaps a different attitude
within them, certainly trying to introduce different working practices'.

The pay-offs are seen as increased flexibility, improved
skills and reduced demarcations. A key tenet of the whole
new 'harmonized' organization is 'a commitment to training on both sides: we want to improve people's skills and
flexibilities and to make things more efficient. In return for
that and in return for us enhancing the pay levels, we
expect people to undergo training, and that's quite firm. If

someone refuses to undergo reasonable training to undertake a reasonable job, we consider that to be quite a serious breakdown in principles.'

Improving communication

Linked with the use of PRP to promote cultural change was the view that the messages it conveyed were of prime importance, and a popular way of looking at PRP was in terms of what it communicated. For example, 'It gives people a clear statement of what is required,' and 'It sends a message to everybody that somebody performing better than another will get paid more, and if he keeps it up, year in, year out, his salary will keep increasing.'

Moreover all respondents saw PRP as having a positive impact on communications, if only because it encouraged or reinforced the appraisal system. For example, one interviewee said, 'In so far as PRP reinforces setting objectives and appraisal, it improves communications, because there is a bigger demand from individuals if they are properly appraised.' Another manager said of a manual appraisal scheme, 'I guess, in that you are forcing the foreman and the supervisor to sit down with each of their subordinates each year, it gives formal access, it forces a formal meeting to happen which, hopefully, should improve communications.'

Yet, as these and other managers said, improving communications was not really one of the fundamental aims behind the introduction of PRP. However, it had proved to be an important side benefit.

Improving recruitment and retention

As was said earlier, increasing motivation in the sense of making people work harder or even 'smarter' was perhaps a less important reason for the introduction of PRP than rewarding good performers. PRP had also been introduced to motivate people to stay with the organization – and in several cases firms appeared to have halted a loss of scarce professionals. In parts of the civil service this appears to have been an important reason for PRP's introduction.

Retention was certainly a key issue for one company. 'Retention is double-edged: we wanted to make sure our high performers were not going to leave us for reasons of salary, or that, if they were, it was going to be quite painful for them. But the other side is that our not-so-good performers did not have so much of a golden handcuff to make them stay with us – they could in fact find another job with another company.' So far as recruitment was concerned, one respondent said, 'We felt that it had become part of the package that young managers expected.'

Individualizing employee relations

Greater individual responsibility was an underlying theme in several of the interviews, but only two of the firms visited had made individual appraisal-based pay the explicit centre of their employee relations philosophy. Because the policy of one of these companies also illustrates most of the themes discussed above, it merits an extensive case study to conclude this chapter.

CASE STUDY 7: ABANDONING THE COST-OF-LIVING PHILOSOPHY

The firm, founded in the early 1980s, forged a distinctive personnel policy based on individualizing employee relations, with the philosophy that 'individuals very much contribute to organizations in different ways and in different amounts. This needed recognizing in some way if you were to motivate people to perform at their best. So the concept of rewarding people for performance and performance-based pay was actually born very early on.'

Performance-based pay is seen as likely to cost more

than a collectively bargained incremental system (the company is not unionized), and hence is justified on the 'grounds of motivation and achievement. . . . It sets the style of an organization, because it says: this is the way we actually treat a person – we look at you as an individual, we look at you in terms of what you are doing for the company. It is almost as important to say that and do some things around it as the actual output.'

PRP is seen as adding to cost, because, for it to be effective, you have to pay the 'over-achievers', as the company calls them, considerably more than those whose performance is acceptable. 'Ultimately you are talking about giving more. You are probably not talking about taking it away from those who have done an acceptable job. So I think you have to put more into it. I don't think you take it away from one group to give to the other.'

High performers can get twice the increase of average performers in any one year. As the interviewee put it, 'I have tried to force the thing to make it mean more, because if I flog my guts out to get an extra one per cent it's not worth it. I have spoken to people who have actually said, "We like coming to work here because there is actually an opportunity to get rewarded for what you do." If you are going to use money as a motivator, you have got to make a difference so over-achievers do actually get significantly more.'

Yet no assumption is made that money is the only motivator. 'I think it's fairly low down the list, and you have to get it right for it to work as a motivator. If everything else is wrong it will not motivate, and if it is wrong other things will cease to be motivators.'

Management prefer to refer to the system as a market-based/merit-driven approach. 'It's market-based because we are very interested to know what other employers will pay for a similar level of job, because we're competing in that labour market. We need to be able to attract and retain people. And it's merit-driven because we want to reward and motivate – that's the correct way round, because you reward someone for something that's gone to motivate them to do better in the future.'

As such the firm does not directly recognize cost of living. 'We say that cost of living is a factor which influences the other [labour] market factors like location, demand and supply – other employers competing for labour. All those are threats, so it means there could be a situation where the cost of living is actually static but the demand is rising considerably, so we have to respond to the market pressure, not the cost of living.'

Although there was no general job evaluation initially in the company, there were pay ranges. But by 1987 nobody really paid much attention to them. 'If you wanted to recruit somebody outside the pay range, you did. If you wanted to pay somebody beyond it, you did.' As the pay ranges appeared to serve no real purpose, the personnel department concluded that they should be abandoned. So in 1987 the company just 'did not include them in the update of the management manual, and no one seemed to notice their passing'.

The procedure for the annual pay award, which is made on 1 May every year, begins with the personnel department producing a report which is sent to all regional managers outlining what is actually being paid within the company for particular groups of employees. This is seen as important, 'to let everybody know what is happening throughout all the regions'. The second part of the procedure is gathering detailed information on what is happening externally, gained either by participating in surveys or by purchasing the results of other surveys. Information is acquired for the full range of occupations and jobs within the company. The justification for this is that 'if you are actually saying you are going to have a market-based approach, you've got to give it some credibility'.

This information-gathering requires significant resources, but was compared favourably with the alternative. 'If we weren't doing that, and I had some sort of union environment, I would probably have about four or five people researching things in order to develop arguments against the unions. Whatever approach I took with pay I would have a lot of people administering it. I might have people involved in job evaluating.'

In collecting market information the firm is trying, not to assert the market rate for each job, but to get an understanding of the labour market and the range of pay. 'The worst term in my view is "market rate". There is no such thing as a rate. "Rate" implies "one", and we know there is a whole range of pay operating out there. If you are matching anything to a market, it is best to throw away the top and the bottom, anyway.'

The aim of the company is for every job holder to perform at a level between the median and the upper quartile of the company pay range, with higher performers at the higher end. Adequate performers should be at the company's median to lower quartile, which will be around the median of the market. 'Generally we would hope to be able to recruit around the median of the market. We want it arranged so that people we are recruiting come in at the lower end of what we pay, and they actually develop in the job and move up.'

Having gathered the market information, the report on it is seen first by top management, who decide that in broad terms the payroll bill and the ranges should increase by a certain percentage. Individuals' pay is then allocated on the basis of where their salary sits in relation to the market and their performance appraisal.

The standard appraisal form contains two elements – one is an appraisal against pre-set objectives, another is a single rating by the appraiser of a person's performance over the year. Managers can choose which type they use, or even use both. The tendency is for people at the lower end of the organization to be simply rated, while those at the higher end are appraised against objectives. 'It is easier to set objectives at a higher level, because people have more individual impact on the achievement of the organization than they do at a lower level. For example, it's more difficult to give an installation engineer objectives over a year because each job is very similar.'

Regardless of the method used, each individual is given an overall rating on a scale of 0–10, with 5–6 representing the standard performance, i.e. meeting the basic requirements of the job. There is no forced or predetermined distribution, and guidelines are not circulated about the distribution – but in practice, typically, 75 per cent are in the 5 and 6 categories, with twice as many 6s as 5s. Twenty per cent are in the 7s and 8s, and 5 per cent are rated 3s and 4s. Ratings 1 and 2, and 9 and 10, are virtually unused.

Having got these ratings, individual pay increases are determined. 'The starting point is not the size of the increase; the starting point is where they are in the market. If someone is sitting at the right part of the market, as judged by the manager, in relation to their performance rating, then you might only give them a small increase, or an increase that matches the market. For achieving the requirements of the job people sit around the median of the market, and our higher achievers should ultimately sit on the upper quartile. If I've got people who are judged to be over-achieving and are low in the market, then I will give them an increase that not only moves them with the market, because that market is moving all the time, but will actually make them move further up the market. If I've got someone who is already at the top and is over-achieving, then I will give him the increase to maintain that position. If I've got people who are at the top and consistently over a period of time are judged to be only achieving the requirements of the job, they almost start moving down. I don't mean taking money away from them – as the market's moving, you might give them an increase which was less than the market movement, to start adjusting their position. But that would only happen over a period of time. We wouldn't automatically drop somebody right back down.'

The main area targeted for further development is to apply a Total Quality approach to objective-setting. The aim is to improve the quality of measurement and to get away from simply judging whether individuals have done certain things, towards assessing the effects of those things: 'measuring output more in terms of what has really been achieved'. An example given was that of using customers' perceptions as a measure of performance. Thus 'if you are actually talking about meeting customer expectations or exceeding them you don't have to worry about subjective measures of quality'.

The reasons for the rise of performance-related pay

- If piecework can be a great motivator but has uncertain results, particularly in a complex, modern service and quality-dependent market, group incentives often fail to focus on the contribution of the individual, while incremental systems fail to reward achievement and give no incentive to those who have reached the ceiling.
- PRP is argued to have all the strengths and none of the weaknesses of the other systems. Individually-based, a rewarder and a motivator, a supporter of organizational, cultural, skill and objective-based change and performance – and capable of relating pay in individual organizations to pay in the outside market.

5

Performance-related pay: key questions

PRP is very different from the earlier forms of incentive schemes, because it relates more to the evolution of Management by Objectives. It starts with the need to achieve targets – through performance improvement systems – in the relatively long term (usually a twelve-month period) rather than in the short term. In this PRP is similar to profit-related bonuses, but the specific targets to which PRP applies usually relate to individuals and not to groups, let alone the organization as a whole. And the focus is often on 'big objectives' or outputs rather than on inputs such as skill and teamwork.

Individual PBR, MDW and group PBR are basically concerned with effort and output. In good times and bad, bonuses can be earned. Group profit-sharing and company-wide bonus schemes generally relate to total output and profit. While bonuses may rise when output is high, they tend to fall when the organization hits a bad patch, whatever the effort being expended by individual workers. PRP can be different. When the organization is doing well, some individuals may receive small bonuses because they achieve little while trying hard (and vice versa). Conversely, when the organization is doing badly some individuals who are judged to have achieved much may be rewarded comparatively well.

While some of the six possible aims of pay systems set out in Chapter 1 are clearly relevant to PRP, not all of them are. The interviews show that it is not usually a prime objective to provide an edge in the labour market, but that PRP does offer a rationale for rewarding individuals who, as high achievers, may otherwise look outside to other employers who offer PRP. On the other hand, some employers specifically include a 'market rate' element when fixing and reviewing PRP. It can be an influence on improving quality, but only to the extent that quality issues are defined in personal objectives. PRP is very strongly associated with changing the culture in an organization and with greater individual responsibility. Co-operation within the work force, teamwork, improvements in skill and greater flexibility may be encouraged by PRP if they are required objectives.

This chapter looks at the evidence of PRP's success in its own terms rather than against the wider objectives. It asks what evidence there is that PRP improves performance, and works as a motivator. It looks at the difficulties of defining individual performance. It asks about the effects of splitting work forces into achievers and non-achievers. It asks what happens when low economic growth affects people's performance pay.

These questions overlap to some extent – for example, the issue of motivation keeps recurring – but considering the issues discussed in this chapter should help those who want to make sure that PRP works as positively as possible within their own organization. The aim is to give a sense of how well schemes are perceived to be working in practice, the problems some have come up against, and what steps (if any) can be taken to counter such problems. The questions concern:

PRP's effects on individual and organization performance:

- Does it work as a motivator? Can it be a demotivator?
- Does it encourage short-termism?
- What effect does it have on team working?
- Is it appropriate to all organizational cultures?
- Does it really improve performance?

PRP's fairness:

- Can individual performance be measured objectively?
- What about factors outside employees' control?
- Can PRP give rise to sex discrimination?

PRP's links with financial and performance management:

- What are its effects on pay costs?
- How can its proper distribution be reconciled with budgetary control?
- How closely is it linked with performance management systems?

Even if some of these questions may be of a rather leading nature, they need answering, if only because in the 1980s so many organizations placed such high expectations on PRP. Are these expectations justified? And if expectations are not always realized, what can be done to make PRP work better?

Individual and organizational performance

Does PRP work as a motivator? Can it be a demotivator?

As a motivator
The personnel managers interviewed for this book were by no means certain that PRP schemes succeeded in motivating people. Most were not convinced they could unequivocally confirm that PRP was increasing either individual or overall organizational performance. Some put it in terms such as 'It's an article of faith.' Or, as a public-sector manager put it, 'We have no clear evidence either way on whether our schemes improve motivation and morale by rewarding good performance, or whether they serve to demotivate employees who are not motivated.' Another

pointed out that, traditionally, the greatest motivator was promotion, and it was still probably the most important.

In particular, there was widespread uncertainty about the precise role of money, and particularly of the effects on motivation of the relatively small levels of monetary inducement entailed in most PRP schemes. Only one manager held the view strongly that money was of prime importance: 'I think money motivates. I think that's what bonus schemes do, they motivate people, because they think they can earn more money and they make them concentrate on the things the business thinks are important. If you've only got so many hours in the day, and you do this or that, and this affects your bonus and that doesn't, you're likely to do this.'

Others had more ambiguous views. A typical response was: 'We obviously consider money to be a motivator in support of performance and management schemes. If not, we wouldn't use it. Perhaps, though, with some reservations. How much of it is money? There is generally a feeling that, if you pay money to people who are generally considered to be striving, this meets people's general view of fairness and equity.' Others felt that 'Up to a certain level it's a motivator. Once a manager has got a certain level of pay and can manage a life style he feels he ought to have, then other things start to come into play.'

One manager, having questioned whether in fact the scheme in his organization made any difference, said, 'But I think there are cases where if there was no merit increase certain managers would be very disappointed, feeling that they had worked extremely hard and had a successful year. It's the Herzberg principle: the real motivation comes from the job, not things like money and the conditions under which they work.' Most respondents qualified their view of money as a motivator by saying it was only one of several factors. PRP was seen as also motivating by giving recognition, feedback and clear direction; money would motivate if the targets set were realistic and achievable, especially if there was no pay increase 'of right' and everything had to be earned in terms of performance.

In one organization which was privatized in the 1980s it was suggested that money might become more important as job security became more threatened. 'Money is not the main motivator, just one of many. We used to be a large company offering job security, career progression and good rates of pay. Now that people are feeling less secure, maybe pay will become more important.' Another interviewee said, 'There are so many factors to motivation. It all depends on the threat at the time. If your job is insecure, then job security is the biggest motivator you can get.'

The issue of whether money motivated related, for some, to the type of person employed and/or their individual circumstances. However, none of the interviewees took their views on the motivational effects of money to what might be seen as a logical conclusion by suggesting that they looked to recruit the sort of people who might be motivated mainly by money for certain jobs, and people who might be motivated by different factors for other jobs.

For others, it was more a question of the amount at stake. For money to be effectively used to change the performance of higher-level members of the organization substantially, it had to be, according to almost all the managers interviewed, a fairly large proportion of salary. The issue for them was not how much of it had to be at risk – i.e. a matter of negative reward – but rather whether the additional money would yield qualitatively different spending power. As one put it, 'If it does not affect the life style, it's not significant.'

In making these judgements, the managers interviewed were heavily influenced by their own attitudes to pay. As one put it, 'For money to become a big incentive/motivator, it must be 10 per cent and probably nearer 20 per cent above for it to make a real difference to what I do.' In his company, with the exception of a sales bonus, none of the systems of pay did this. The same was true of the majority of the PRP schemes in the firms studied.

Several interviewees felt that, once monetary reward was at a satisfactory level, recognition became the major factor. Recognition was usually defined along the lines, 'that somebody feels you are doing a good job'. As one put it, 'If there is good basic pay, then recognition is the greatest motivator – especially feedback on performance from the manager.' Or, as one public-sector manager reported, 'What has been found to be a motivator has been the actual feedback you've got on performance and the fact that if somebody said to you, "You are in band 2," it means something.'

Money and recognition were not, however, totally unrelated. The two were perceived to be linked. 'They say, "You've met your objectives – here's ten thousand quid." You've not only got recognition, you have greater clarity about your objectives, why objectives are here and why you are being paid.' To quote one manager, 'Money is the reinforcer of the underlying philosophy. The business is saying that we must strive to get business up, reduce costs, and we don't reward the under-performer.'

Some respondents saw the way payment systems were operated as a help in creating commitment by developing in employees favourable views of their organization. If the PRP schemes were operated fairly, and were seen to be so, this could leave employees, so some interviewees said, well disposed towards the company. In so far as PRP did this, it could be motivating, or at least, 'it eliminates things which can interfere with motivation'.

However, references made to employees looking favourably on PRP schemes were very much in terms of equity, and not just in terms of money as a motivator. For example, one manager at corporate head office of a large financial services organization reported that their experience was that PRP 'was increasingly being welcomed. But, I must say, in a rather negative way: it is not that people are motivated to work harder in order to get more money, it is more that they are content about working harder if they think that other people who work less hard are getting less than they are.'

In the public sector there was definitely more questioning of the role of money in motivation. One interviewee from the National Health Service believed that PRP was not a motivator, because 'by and large people are not working in the Health Service for the money'. She argued that this view was borne out by a communications survey carried out by an external consultant in her health authority which revealed that job satisfaction was the main motivator. Other motivators included 'doing something worthwhile' and working with people. The results of the survey were the same for senior managers as they were for lower-level participants.

One study focusing on the motivational impact of PRP in the public sector was carried out among 2,500 Inland Revenue staff for the Inland Revenue Staff Federation (IRSF) by Marsden and Richardson from the London School of Economics (1991). The study covered Inland Revenue grades represented by the IRSF and was not confined to union members. The main findings were that Revenue staff generally supported the principle of PRP but that a significant minority felt hostile to it; and that the positive motivational effects of PRP had been, at most, very modest and felt to any degree by only a small minority of staff. Only 12 per cent said that PRP had raised their motivation; 76 per cent said that it had not. This view was shared by those staff (about 20 per cent of the total sample) who had to carry out staff appraisals, i.e. Reporting Officers. Tables 10 and 11 illustrate these findings in more detail. The researchers suggested that one reason for this failure in motivation was that the allocation of performance payments was seen to be unfair. Many of their respondents felt that the long-standing appraisal system

Table 10 Inland Revenue staff assessment of their own motivational responses to performance pay (%)

Performance pay has led you to:	Yes	No
Improve the quality of your work	12	80
Increase the quality of work	14	78
Work harder	9	71
Work beyond the job requirements	21	70
Give sustained high performance	27	63
Improve your priorities at work	22	64
Show more initiative	27	61
Express yourself with greater clarity	13	67
Be more effective with the public	9	68
Improve your sensitivity towards colleagues	14	63

Source. Marsden and Richardson (1991).

Table 11 The views of Inland Revenue reporting officers on the impact of performance pay on their staff (%)

Performance pay has:	Yes	No
Caused many staff to work beyond the requirements of their job	15	79
Led many staff to give sustained high performance at work	14	77
Helped to increase the quality of the work of many staff	10	82
Led to an increase in the quantity of the work of many staff	22	71
Made many staff more committed to their work	12	79

Source. Marsden and Richardson (1991).

had been distorted and degraded by being tied to decisions about money. Many also believed that a quota on bonus payments was in operation and that it frequently overrode the assessment of performance.

The researchers also found that PRP was most successful in motivating the most junior grades and those with the shortest service, although, even among these groups, most reported no motivational effect. The effects on motivation were generally weakest among the more senior grades and the longer-serving staff. The researchers suggested that this could be because, as a percentage of salary, a PRP award was more valuable to staff on the lower grades, and because many in senior grades have a somewhat different view of their work, with already higher levels of motivation. If this finding were shown to apply in other organizations, it could cast doubt upon one of the conventional wisdoms of PRP: that it should be introduced for senior staff first and gradually extended down the hierarchy.

What about demotivation?
While views about the motivational aspects of PRP were distinctly ambiguous, virtually all the managers interviewed considered that PRP could be a demotivator for those not getting high pay increases.

Yet through all the interviews there was only one instance where the demotivating effect of PRP had caused management to amend the scheme. The problem had arisen because the firm classified people into four bands and predetermined the numbers to be covered by each band. The effect was that 80 per cent were classified either in band 3 or in band 4, and consequently saw themselves as labelled 'average' or below.* Moreover, when the company had first introduced the scheme it had talked in terms of motivation in its publicity and in the briefings about it. Subsequent feedback had told management that this was demotivating, because the implication was that senior management felt people were not already motivated. As a result the banding system was abandoned, the

---

* If it is true, as research suggests, that most people rate themselves 'above average' (although logically that cannot be true), labelling the bulk of employees as 'average' or worse looks like a recipe for demotivation!

language was amended so as to use more positive terms, and greater emphasis was put on changing the organizational culture through performance-related pay. The LSE survey of Inland Revenue staff also found negative motivational effects arising from PRP, as shown in Table 12.

Table 12 Inland Revenue staff views on some effects of performance pay on staff as a whole (%)

Performance pay has:	Yes	No
Helped to undermine staff morale	55	25
Caused jealousies between staff	62	21
Made staff less willing to assist colleagues	26	53

Source. Marsden and Richardson (1991).

Some firms consciously aimed not to reward the exceptional or high performers disproportionately. One organization, for example, assumed that most people would get the middle grade, C, and wanted to make sure that the average performer was able to achieve a certain level of recognition. So the company rejected a philosophy of 'giving massive pay rises to the very high performers and very mediocre pay rises to Mr Joe Average. Instead the management felt that Joe Average should also have a reasonable level of award,' otherwise PRP could end up by demotivating 80 per cent of its people.

Underlying many responses was concern that schemes demotivated those who were not placed at the higher ends of pay or rating scales, whilst the amount of money given to others might be insufficient really to motivate them. The study of the Inland Revenue also suggested that staff felt that the amount of money was not large enough to justify a change in behaviour.

In one public-sector organization the interviewee reported that anybody who got less than the maximum of

6 per cent felt insulted. 'So instead of feeling pleased that they got 3 per cent (the second point) because everybody had recognized their performance was good, they would be demotivated because they had not got the 6 per cent that was excellent.' Several respondents suggested a figure between 15 per cent and 25 per cent as a proportion of salary at risk which might genuinely act as a motivator.

However, it was precisely because effort and business performance might not always coincide that several firms did not want to have too much pay at risk. As one interviewee said, 'We are in a very cyclical business; it can be very volatile. Two years ago the market dropped like a stone, much quicker than anybody could have imagined – then we had the Gulf War, with its external influences. People are probably working harder in those circumstances to mitigate the problems but they will not achieve the objectives which we established at the beginning of the year. And I think if you've got a lot of money riding on that, then it's a kind of roulette situation, which is not very helpful.'

One firm explicitly had a policy of not wanting the senior executives' bonuses to be too high a proportion of salary, 'because the down side of a big bonus is that if you get people used to it, and you get a recession, and that money goes to the good ones, the marketable ones will leave because they are used to getting that money.'

A small bonus is more likely to be seen as an 'extra'. The personnel director of the above firm illustrated it thus: 'In our business, what we have seen this year with our 10 per cent bonus – some of the senior executives feel positively guilty. They said, "The way things are going, we thought you'd withdraw it." So they clearly see it as nice to have. When times are good we should all get 10 per cent, but when times are tough we should not really get it.'

What about average and poor performers?
Several respondents said that the introduction of PRP had
encouraged the identification of poor performers. As one
public-sector manager put it, 'It has meant that people are
being forced to address people who are not performing,
which, to be honest, has been an issue which has been
dodged in the past.' The demotivating effect of low or zero
pay increases on poorly rated people was not perceived by
many as a serious problem. Indeed, in several cases
managers specifically reported welcoming it, on the
grounds that it might 'buck them up', motivate them to
improve or, as in fact was more common, motivate them to
leave.

There was, however, a feeling that PRP was not used
sufficiently to motivate poor performers. In one case (and
it was not an isolated instance) the criticism levelled by
the interviewee at the operation of the scheme pointed not
to the organization abandoning PRP but rather to a
tightening up of the operation of the existing scheme. In
particular he was unsure about the effects of the con-
tinuation of a cost of living element: 'I don't like this. I am
not sure that it's giving the right messages, to go on paying
[a cost of living element] to poor performers.' The message
he particularly wanted to give was 'If you don't perform, it
is going to hit you in the pocket. PRP needs a down side as
well as an up side, and we don't do this enough.'

This respondent felt that line managers were rating too
generously; in his terms, they were a 'soft lot'. The
organization had a five-point rating scale, and though 50
per cent were typically on box 2 (1 is the top), there was a
perception that people getting box 3 – 40 per cent did so –
were likely to feel demotivated, as they received only the
normal increment. Someone on the scale maximum, on
the other hand, whose increase was limited even under
PRP, was likely, in the interviewee's words, to 'plod along
being inefficient, and sit there picking up his cost of living
revision until retirement when he gets his index-linked

pension. The person plods along, not taking advantage of incentives to do well, but we don't have a stick if he doesn't come up to scratch.'

Interviewees' responses tended to focus on the two ends of the performance spectrum. PRP was seen as a device to reward and retain the high performers and to motivate (often to motivate to leave!) the low performers. But there was little reference to the middle range of performers, who may constitute 80 per cent of any organization. Some have obviously given thought to what motivates such people by ensuring that they are included in PRP schemes, but few interviewees seemed to know whether PRP motivated or demotivated them, or whether its impact was simply neutral.

Does PRP work as a motivator? Can it be a demotivator?
- It is a motivator – but only one, if an important one, among many.
- It depends on the amount at stake – should it be a relatively large proportion of pay?
- It can be a demotivator if the money 'isn't right', or if Joe Average doesn't get a share.
- Insufficient consideration may be given to its effects on average performers.
- Other conditions need to be right. People need to feel that a change in behaviour will produce sufficient reward.

Does PRP encourage short-termism?

In one company the possibility of PRP tending to encourage short-termism had become an important issue. 'The senior management and directors' bonus scheme tends to have a short-term impetus which might adversely affect the medium to long term prospects of the business.' The bonus scheme was designed to achieve budgeted profit and is in effect 'an incentive to achieve the single year's profit in isolation and at the expense of building a future'.

This interviewee also offered an example to illustrate the dangers of short-termism. 'You might have to reach a profit target of £x million, and you look three-quarters of the way through the year and you say to yourself, "No way am I going to get this by normal trading. What I'll do is have a sale and I'll make my goods very attractive. I'll reduce them by 20 per cent, which will encourage my customers to stockpile my products." And by doing these things you get a nice fat bonus. But next year the trade is stacked to the gunnels with your products and next time they want to buy they say, "Don't tell me your prices are so much. You let me have that for £8 last time. Now you say it's £10 and you have to give me a discount." It might be £9, but your margin is attacked. That's a real problem.'

Other interviewees expressed similar concern, and some organizations had taken steps to tackle them. For example, in reviewing its salesmen's bonuses one firm was concerned that they were neglecting the development of relations with customers to make a 'fast buck'. As the interviewee put it, 'We've started to ask, "Do we just want our salesmen to sell, or do we want them to make a fuss of the customer?" Customer care, and all that sort of thing.' The problem with this, though, the interviewee continued, was that 'performance becomes less quantifiable'.

Only a few organizations had pursued the logic of these concerns and introduced specific long-term objectives, although one interviewee from the public sector talked of the ability to set three-year objectives to run alongside shorter-term targets. One example from the private sector was of a company which had introduced a long-term incentive plan for its top forty managers based on the growth of earnings per share over a four-year period. If the target for this was achieved over the period, a bonus would be paid of twice annual salary for directors and of one year's salary for the remaining senior managers.

For some managers short-termism was not, however, perceived as a problem, precisely because individual objectives are set in the light of business plans. An example of a longer-term approach to objectives and rewards was given by a manager in a financial services organization. 'A chief executive of one of the business units was given the task of getting his administrative systems right, and his boss told him, "Don't worry about increasing profit this year – just keep profits ticking over. Concentrate on getting your administration right so you can make profits in the future." A key objective for this year became overhauling the administration, and it was a major part of the person's appraisal.'

One company, worried that bonuses for area sales managers based on performance targets might lead to short-termism, tried to offset this by giving them in addition a set of core managerial activities. These included appraisal, staff development and customer care.

Does PRP encourage short-termism?
- Some ill-thought-out schemes may have adversely affected the medium and long-term well-being of businesses.
- Steps can be taken to discourage this, for example by introducing long-term (but sometimes less quantifiable) objectives.

What effect does PRP have on team working?

In around half the interviews the possible negative effect of PRP and bonuses on team-building was acknowledged. As one interviewee put it, 'It is a bit of a down side. Some staff in our organization argue PRP is actually detrimental to team working because people are assessed as an individual and work for an increase almost in competition with their colleagues.' In one case it was reported that one group of employees (in the mail room) had actually asked their manager to give everyone the same increase to avoid internal conflict. In another company the senior managers' targets were imposed on them, having been devised by the chief executive from the business plan and given to them in a way which encouraged them 'to get their heads down and singularly go for their own objectives without regard to others'.

There seemed to be a feeling in some public-sector organizations that PRP was driving people to achieve objectives regardless of the cost in terms of co-operation. As one respondent put it, 'PRP was seen as not helping team working, and indeed one of the stated intentions behind its introduction was that there is a competitive element to it.'

Often, however, individual bonuses or PRP and team working are not seen as antithetical, and sometimes bonuses are determined by a mixture of individual and group incentives. Interviewees reported how increasing teamwork and team-building are often included in managers' objectives. One said, 'If it [PRP] does cut across team working, then there is something wrong with the target-setting or the appraisal.' In one case (a senior executive bonus scheme) each manager's targets were set in conjunction with each other's, and each manager was deliberately given at least one objective which another had too. All the executives were involved in this target-setting process. It was claimed that the introduction of the bonus scheme, two years ago, had increased team-building and that collective working made managers focus on broader objectives than those of their own function.

A different view of the relationship between PRP and team working was provided by another respondent. 'I think we encourage people to work in teams because that's part of our working atmosphere and we don't necessarily reward them to work in teams, that's taken as read. What we want is for them to give their individual utmost to team work, so, by encouraging people to work as individuals, that tends to generate good team performance as well.'

PRP was seen by one manager as positively encouraging team-building by providing clear objectives. 'PRP has had considerable impact on co-operation and team-building. Again, because we've got greater clarity, you've got an acceptance that you need to be clear on what is wanted and what fits which part of the puzzle where, and to have greater awareness of what different managers are doing.'

There were some examples of schemes which had been abandoned because of the difficulty of attributing good or bad performance to individuals. For example, to cope with the problems of rewarding, attracting and retaining investment analysts following deregulation, an insurance company had introduced a complex individual bonus scheme based on individual targets. It subsequently abandoned the scheme in favour of an objectives-based approach similar to a scheme introduced for other employees, because of the difficulty of attributing success to any one individual.

One retailer preferred group bonuses to individual commission on the assumption that a 'good sales team, pulling together' could increase sales. Group bonuses also dealt with the problem of customers 'reconnaissance shopping', when one shop assistant is spoken to initially but the sale is finalized by a different assistant on a different day.

What effect does PRP have on team working?
- This is a real concern. Several organizations acknowledged that PRP can have a negative effect on team working by overemphasizing incentives for the individual
- As long as the basic measure of performance is not exclusively individually based, this can be countered by including team-building and teamwork in objectives.

Is PRP appropriate to all organizational cultures?

Some, although by no means all, public-sector organizations (and certainly most of the public-sector unions) have
expressed disquiet at the spread of PRP on the grounds that
it is inappropriate to the idea of public service. For
example, a local authority officer said, 'If you have an
organization which has service to the public as a major
plank in its culture, that doesn't fit comfortably with the
sort of highly financially motivated, driven approach
which obviously is felt to work by those who are involved
in business. Obviously in a business context the prime
measure of performance is going to be profit, and the
concept of sharing in the results of the bonuses I think
actually hangs together much more logically than performance-related pay in local government, which is actually
grafted on to a very different sort of value system.'
However, other public-sector interviewees found aspects
of PRP valuable, particularly its role in reinforcing appraisal systems.

Perhaps the real issue is whether PRP should be used by
itself to effect the sorts of cultural change referred to in the
previous chapter – for example, to make organizations
more customer or performance-oriented – or whether it
needs to be combined with other changes (which might
perhaps be introduced ahead of PRP). Putting the question
the other way round, how far does PRP have to fit the
prevailing culture to be successful?

Is PRP appropriate to all organizational cultures?
- This is a concern in some parts of the public sector,
  but elsewhere in the public sector aspects of PRP
  are felt to be valuable.
- But PRP alone should not be used to promote
  cultural change.

Does PRP really improve individual or organizational performance?

By and large, personnel managers appeared to rely on informal methods of assessment, based on their involvement in the process, to sense how their schemes were working. Few evaluated the schemes formally and sought evidence of links between the running of a scheme and performance. For example, when talking of the impact of a sales bonus on individual performance, one said it 'cultivates it'. Another, asked about the impact of PRP on output and individual performance, said, 'I have no straightforward way of answering.'

Most managers were not convinced that they could pinpoint the effect of PRP on individual or overall organizational performance. One said, 'I don't have any way of assessing it, and I can't conceive of one.' For some – especially in the service sector – there were clearly difficulties in measuring output and individual performance. Many organizations, in both the public and the private sectors, did not appear to have very reliable measures of output or of individual performance.

In some situations the relationship between individual performance and company performance can seem problematic if an employer has no clearly thought out objectives. A good example is the processing of insurance claims. If individual performance were assessed on speed in processing claims, and employees were paid on that basis, it could increase the flow of funds out of the firm. As an interviewee in one large insurance firm said, 'They could be working five times harder than usual, but effectively they are giving our money away. How could you reward them in the case of storm damage?' Using PRP for such staff was viewed as 'very difficult'.

Managers freely admitted that they did not evaluate pay systems. One manager, who had introduced performance appraisal for production workers, said, 'I don't think we have actually looked at its success, partly perhaps because we might not want to know the results.' Another respondent in the insurance industry just sensed that PRP was working. 'I don't think there is anything measurable by which we can judge the impact of PRP on performance; because of all the external factors – hurricanes, etc. – it's much more to do with effective management, as seen by the top management, than anything else.'

Some managers were sceptical about being able to evaluate PRP in any decisive way. As one personnel manager in a firm which had just introduced PRP argued, 'The fundamental problem we have is that you can't compare [what we have done] with how it would have been had we not done it.' Another argued, 'It's difficult for me to tell, because I haven't seen the alternative, and I'm not in the sort of game where it's easy to assess things – it's not like a production line [where] you could say that under the old system we used to produce 100 cans a day and now we produce 110 cans a day. I can't tell you that, and anyway the situation is changing all the time.'

Monitoring schemes
Some managers based their judgements on more concrete evidence, either from exit interviews or from attitude surveys. For example, one said, 'We carry out exit interviews and [these show that employees'] primary interests are the challenge of the job, job content and job interest. The pay has to be right, but after that it is other factors that count. Money is a secondary motivator.'

Many PRP schemes have monitoring built in; personnel departments co-ordinate all the appraisals and projected increases before they are agreed by senior management. Often the personnel department may query certain suggested payments prior to their being finalized; for example, if the appraisal does not square with the pay. In this way the personnel function acts as what one interviewee called an umpire, trying to guarantee consistency and reducing the number of demotivated people. As one manager recalled, 'For example, we had a situation a few years ago when a manager was very tight in his allocation of merit pay and we had to lean on him to be fairer. He did not even attempt to use the allowable increase in the salary budget. He expected more from his people than perhaps the average manager would have done. That was obviously going to be a very demotivating factor for the people involved.'

It was difficult to establish the precise nature and extent of the monitoring of schemes in the organizations visited. In some cases statistics are compiled – for example, breaking down pay increases by gender, ethnicity, length of service and education level. In one company, the compensation department does a report each year on the way the salary review has gone and comments on the variability of scoring from one department to another. This is fed back to departments. Another firm, having just introduced PRP, planned to interview a selection of managers and employees about the conduct of appraisals and any problems arising from it. In this firm, as in others, all the appraisal forms are sent to the personnel department after the pay round, so the personnel function can discuss with the appraisers any particular career needs or problems expressed on the forms.

Attitude surveys
In the interview programme only one example was found of a company which regularly uses attitude surveys to ascertain the views of employees. There were two sources: a remuneration opinion survey and a general opinion survey. The following questions have been drawn from one of the surveys to illustrate the sort of questions which can be asked:

• How well do you feel the company is doing in matching pay to performance?

- To what extent do you agree with your manager's appraisal of your performance?
- What is your view as to your last pay increase in relation to the percentage available and your performance?
- I am clear about the results expected of me doing my job.
- I agree with my manager's appraisal of my performance.
- The most important factor upon which salary increases should be based (the choices were: experience; performance; potential; hard work and commitment; internal relativities; the external market place).

Does PRP improve individual or organizational performance?
- Few organizations have formally evaluated PRP schemes. While they believe PRP does improve individual or organizational performance, they find it difficult to substantiate this view.
- Exit interviews, the compilation and comparison of performance statistics between departments, and attitude surveys, can help to provide evidence of how schemes are working.

PRP and fairness

Can individual performance be measured objectively?

Problems of setting objectives
One of the most commonly quoted problems with PRP is the objective-setting process. In the interviews, personnel managers reported how their line managers, often very new to setting targets, had sometimes said how difficult they found setting objectives which were, in the words of one, 'challenging but not unachievable, and so payments are motivating rather than demotivating'.

The problem of objective-setting seems especially acute

in the public sector, which until recently has not appeared to make extensive use of Management by Objectives. The Council of Civil Service Unions (CCSU), in a submission to a National Audit Office inquiry into the civil service appraisal scheme, said, 'The CCSU accepts that staff need to know what is expected of them. However, we doubt whether objective-setting is realistic in the case of some grades and posts, and there are genuine fears that it is being used simply to ratchet up productivity. There is too much of a focus on quantity to the exclusion of quality. We are concerned also that the setting of unrealistic objectives may lead to disciplinary action on inefficiency grounds' (quoted in Labour Research Department, 1990). And one local authority personnel manager revealed, 'We are finding that managers are not very good at defining measurable targets and how to set realistic ones. Some targets are too easy and some too difficult.' There is also the problem that there are some jobs in which there is an opportunity to shine, while in others there is less opportunity – described by one public-sector interviewee as 'the full-back/centre forward syndrome'.

Underlying the move to objective-setting was the worry that some managers were setting easy, not hard, targets. Another problem reported is inconsistency between managers, some setting softer targets than others. The fear of soft objectives being set was not, however, one which all managers shared. For example, one put it this way: 'There is no danger of soft objectives, because they are related to the business plan, and the business plan is never a soft target.' To achieve fairness and objectivity, in certain organizations each appraiser is overseen by his or her superior. For example, each person appraised may be given both a 'parent' (the immediate superior) and a 'grandparent' (usually the superior's immediate superior) who actually see all the objectives of their subordinates to assess whether they are reasonable. (This is not seen as a complete answer. Senior managers are often insufficiently familiar with operational details to be able to pass such judgements.)

In schemes which do not use objectives, managers are often given guidelines setting out the kinds of criteria by which they should judge subordinates. But in other cases it is left to managers to decide the criteria themselves. As an interviewee in such a situation said, 'It's up to the manager, but I suppose managers consider how they've performed, how they've done their job, what their attendance has been like, to what extent they've met targets, and so on.'

Most firms seemed to want to have quantitative measurable objectives, and hence were especially attracted to financial targets. (Clearly, this may be more difficult in the public sector, although not always.) As one manager in a company which gives priority to such objectives put it: 'If something matters sufficiently to the business that it is a key objective, then it matters to find a way to measure it.' The danger of this approach, which the interviewer acknowledged, is that managers may shy away from objectives which are not readily measurable. The particular firm was facing up to the fact that, compared with all its world-wide competitors, its performance over the past ten years had been very poor. Consequently the desire to quantify objectives 'fitted in with the present approach, which is to compare the firm's performance with others', to isolate the causes of the problems'.

Participation in objective-setting by the individuals being assessed does not appear to be something which firms consider absolutely necessary for successful performance management. But, equally, few if any impose objectives from above. The process of goal-setting seems in general to be a process initiated by superiors but involving 'some discussion', as several respondents put it, between superiors and subordinates.

The most commonly perceived administrative problem, or potential problem, is setting objectives in time. In one case the interviewee actually began by saying, 'I've not had mine set yet.' The first year of his firm's new scheme was supposed to have started five weeks before. The problem of getting objectives out on time is not a simple question of managerial competence or speed of response: if managers aim to link individual targets and objectives with overall business plans, the determination of those objectives must await the publication of the business plan.

Appraisal
PRP linked to objective-setting implies the use of some form of appraisal, although if all the objectives are financial targets (as in many senior executive bonus schemes) then there is no necessary reason for an appraisal: the payment can be formula-based.

The study of Inland Revenue staff found that 87 per cent felt that 'PRP had made staff question the fairness of the appraisal system'; 63 per cent believed that 'a good appraisal is too often overruled by someone higher up'; and 35 per cent felt that 'people get a good box marking not so much because of their performance but because managers want to reward their favourites'. Findings like these led the researchers to conclude not only that there was widespread doubt about the fairness of the appraisal system but that PRP, in being bolted on to a well established appraisal system, had undermined it. The personnel managers interviewed for this report were clearly aware of these sorts of potential problems: one of the reported difficulties with appraisals was that, whilst 'managers may be trained in the procedures and encouraged to observe correct marking standards', they have their own agenda and feel more comfortable being generous to the lower performers than rewarding the high performers. Managers can also set easily attainable objectives, or phrase them in general terms which make it easy to show that they have been achieved.

A further danger in linking appraisal with the pay

review is that appraisals can turn into individual negotiations, though managers say that the danger is minimized if appraisals are based on pre-set objectives. This was a common reason for wishing to move from 'merit pay' systems, under which managers' assessments are not related to the achievement of pre-set objectives.

Generally, formal appraisal systems were said to be working well. In most, through training and monitoring, managers had been encouraged not to concentrate solely on the previous year's performance but to discuss personal development and to identify training needs. Some appraisal forms had two distinct sections, one dealing with past performance, the other with developmental needs.

However, one manager argued that, because the bottom categories of scales are rarely used, PRP and appraisals were not fully effective. He thought that this practice was difficult to reverse. Because less than 5 per cent of employees were placed in the lowest category it became associated with abject failure and people being singled out. But, he argued, if a larger proportion – he suggested the figure of 30 per cent – were placed in lower bands they would not be regarded (or regard themselves) as being singled out and 'managers could use it as a constructive category'.

Some firms were attempting to counter the problem by separating the timing of the appraisal/performance review from the salary review. The appraisal could then provide an input to the salary review. One firm contemplating introducing PRP to replace its incremental system envisaged keeping appraisal separate. As its compensation manager put it, 'Appraisal is so important in its own right. It has immense value in itself and it should not be bastardized by linking it to pay.' One of the reasons for maintaining a separate appraisal scheme in this case was that management wanted the trade unions to be involved in the process. They were seen as having a contribution to make to the improvement of the process, its redesign, selling it to employees, and even in bringing recalcitrant managers (i.e. those who did not take appraisal seriously) into line. Appraisal was seen as having considerable value, particularly in terms of providing recognition for individuals, and identifying development needs.

Can individual performance be measured objectively?
- Especially for those who are not used to doing so, it can be difficult to set measurable and realistic targets, particularly where financial targets cannot be used or are inappropriate.
- It can be difficult to achieve consistency between managers, both in terms of setting targets and in terms of appraising people.
- PRP thus puts a new emphasis on the effectiveness of appraisal. This requires training and monitoring.
- Some organizations attempt to counter problems of appraisal being turned into negotiating sessions by separating the performance review from the pay review.

What about factors outside employees' control?

Changes outside individuals' control, happening after targets or objectives have been set and sending them off course, are acknowledged to create problems. An example of an environmental change creating problems of measuring performance was offered by a manager in a pharmaceutical firm. 'The classic occasion occurs when we have a sales target or a market share to achieve, and our competitor releases a new product on to the market.' Another case is the influence of the recession on retail sales, resulting in managers having to work harder than ever to offset its adverse effects. One company tried to overcome the problem by awarding one-off bonuses which were not permanent additions to salary (and hence were non-pensionable) to people who had done exceptionally well in difficult circumstances. As the manager there put it, 'Someone may have worked very hard but failed to achieve his targets owing to factors totally beyond his control.'

The problem of performance-related bonus schemes in a recession raises the question of whether sales bonuses are in fact fair-weather schemes. One personnel manager in a retail firm which aims to motivate people through sales bonuses linked to target volumes said, 'Sales volume is crucial: if the Chancellor puts 2 per cent on interest rates people don't buy furniture, and profit targets really do go out of the window early in the year. Then incentives become irrelevant.'

This manager – and he was not alone – believed that it was almost inevitable that motivation would be affected by downturns if pay were linked to performance. As he put it, 'In a sense it's paradoxical. Very often when bonuses are doing badly and people are working twice as hard to achieve anything it's usually when they are not going to get bonus – and I think that's depressing and a shame. If you lower the targets it raises another question: can the business afford to pay a bonus?' The dangers of pay not being adequately linked with effort highlighted for the manager concerned 'why it's important to have the base pay right against the market'. It also raises the question whether, at least in some organizations, PRP may be really a form of profit-related pay.

Factors apparently beyond individuals' control were not, however, seen as valid reason to make allowances for under-achievement. Apart from the harm which can be caused by paying bonus when the organization is doing badly, there may be less obvious links between individual performance and results. To illustrate this, one public sector manager who gave 'the government cutting off funding for the project you are working on' as an example of a factor beyond an individual's control, added that 'This may reflect the failure of the people inside the organization to convince the customer of its merits.' A retailing firm using bonuses for senior managers and sales staff took the view that, despite recessions and weather conditions affecting demand, 'sales could in fact be generated'. Their bonus scheme was based on the assumption that, by putting effort into helping and initiating contact with customers, people could increase sales above what they might otherwise have achieved.

The problem of outside influences did not carry much weight in another organization. Taking exchange rates as the 'classic' example, the interviewee argued, 'Of course managers cannot control them. But we expect exchange rates to influence their budgets and business plans. They should take cognizance of this factor when planning. They have to make judgements about it. We pay them to get it right.' Another interviewee took a slightly softer line: whilst you take account of things which happened beyond the individual's control and 'apply sound judgement' you also 'look at whether the manager took steps to mitigate it or just let it happen'.

In most of the organizations surveyed there was similar scope for flexibility in the operation of many of the procedures. Managers were encouraged quickly to flag up any changes that meant they would be unable to meet their objectives, as one particular objective became irrelevant or another needed to take precedence.

In some cases there were formalized procedures for reviewing objectives throughout the year. For example, 'There are continuous reviews during the year, and formal performance appraisal at the end of the year, so if objectives need to be changed, or reset, that will happen part of the way through the year. If something else comes up that is considered to be more urgent, I have to renegotiate objectives and time scales.'

It is usually intended or formally stated that managers

should meet their subordinates at certain stages of the year to review objectives. However, in practice this did not always happen because 'of pressure of time', as interviewees invariably put it. As one said, reviewing objectives 'can be a lengthy process. Assuming you've got a reasonable boss, then lateness should not affect your assessment.'

A good example of objectives changing to reflect changing circumstances is the way in which one organization relying on quantifiable targets to award bonuses for senior managers had added the reduction of working capital to its prime objective (operating profit) in order to reflect the fact that although sales were down – as they were in the 1990/1 recession – managers could still improve the overall return on capital by reducing stocks and debtors. The company, though not operating a formal individual objective-based PRP scheme linked with an appraisal system, looked at its bonus schemes every year to see whether particular things, e.g. reducing stock in a particular year, should be targeted.

What about factors outside employees' control?
- Downturns in the economy can reduce individuals' performance pay, though they may be working harder to compensate.
- Thus it is important to have the base pay right against the market.
- But people should try to mitigate outside influences, and this can be taken into account when assessing performance.
- Some organizations allow objectives to be reviewed in the light of outside events or changed priorities; others do not encourage this.
- Should people expect less in a recession? Should good performers get less and the average get nothing?

Does PRP give rise to sex discrimination?

At the 1991 Trades Union Congress the Association of
First Division Civil Servants (FDA), the union representing senior civil servants, alleged that official figures
showed that 52 per cent of male civil servants in Grades
Five to Seven qualified for extra performance-related
payments, while only 38 per cent of women did so. This
claim followed an examination of performance awards to
about 16,000 civil servants, taking only those of equal
seniority at the top of the pay scales. The disparities
between men and women were the same for the three
grades, in which women make up about 20 per cent of
employees. At the time of writing the FDA was reported to
be seeking legal advice on whether the pay system was in
breach of European law. However, civil service management said they were satisfied that on the strength of the
information available there was no evidence of discrimination against women generally in the award of
performance pay to staff in Grades Five to Seven and that
any imbalances could be attributed to structural factors.
They also said that, if civil service performance pay
arrangements were extended, it would be important to
install adequate monitoring and review mechanisms in
order to ensure as far as possible that discrimination did
not occur.

In addition, union monitoring of PRP at the insurance
company General Accident showed that, following a
successful appeal to the Central Arbitration Committee,
awards varied between locations and discriminated
against women, part-timers and older workers. Similarly,
union monitoring at British Rail is alleged to have found
wide disparities between different locations, individuals
with the same appraisal rating not infrequently receiving
different awards.

The Equal Opportunities Commission (EOC) has
warned that PRP may discriminate indirectly where it is

limited in its application to grades or sections of the work force in such a way as to exclude women disproportionately, and where PRP is available only after an extended period of service, which women are less likely to achieve. The EOC says that the rights of part-time and temporary workers must be safeguarded if pay is performance-related, and such workers within the job category covered by the scheme must be included. A clause excluding part-timers from a PRP scheme for NHS managers was removed after a complaint to the EOC in 1987.

Public-sector employers are being made aware of the possibility of sex discrimination: in a report published in November 1990 (PRP Report No. 4), the Local Authorities Conditions of Service Advisory Board said, 'So far as the coverage of PRP schemes [in local government] is concerned, they are at present mainly applied to senior employees, who are primarily male, and even where PRP has been extended down the organization more generous payments tend to be available to those at the top of the hierarchy. In many cases, therefore, it is probable that the introduction of PRP will widen internal pay relativities and will also widen the salary gap between male and female local government officers, because of the disproportionate concentration of women in lower grades. It remains to be seen how these arrangements will be viewed under Equal Pay legislation.'

Apart from the General Accident case, all publicized instances of possible sex discrimination appear to have arisen in the public sector and all the cases which have earned publicity have been in unionized environments. In only one of the interviews, where there was explicit monitoring by gender of the results of appraisal, did it emerge that these concerns had surfaced as yet. However, LACSAB's conclusions seem sensible and would appear to be applicable to sectors other than local government. LACSAB argued that, especially where PRP extends below senior management grades and covers an increasing proportion of women, 'It will be advisable for procedures to be developed specifically to monitor the distribution of performance payments between men and women; and to pay specific attention to equal pay in the design of PRP procedures. The operation of an appeals procedure and the involvement of unions in PRP schemes may also help to ensure that equal pay requirements are met. Management need to have awareness and to take positive steps to eliminate discrimination, in order to avoid the possibility of PRP schemes being operated unfairly and to the detriment of women employees.'

Can PRP give rise to sex discrimination?
- Evidence of sex discrimination in the distribution of PRP has been claimed (and in some cases confirmed by an industrial tribunal).
- Procedures to monitor the distribution of performance payments between men and women should be considered by employers.

Financial and performance management

What are PRP's effects on pay costs?

Few interviewees believed that PRP had added to the overall salary bill. In some cases managers said that wage costs might actually have been reduced. In one company, for example, it was reported, 'The overall spend is lower than on the old cost-of-living and merit structure. We have been able to contain costs better, as we save on poor performers.' The company argued that with the improved identification of poor performers, some of whom had left the organization under an early retirement scheme, the total salary bill had gone down, as their replacements had joined on a lower salary. The general conclusion was that the organization got better value for money with performance-related pay. As the interviewee said, 'By rewarding for contribution you are looking at how pay impacts on the bottom line. In other words, if you are paying an extra pound you are getting better performance for it.'

Although some interviewees found it difficult to assess the impact of PRP on the overall salary bill, the general view was that PRP was self-financing, that it had not led to higher overall wages for average performers, and that the linking of pay to performance had meant that 'Managers are much more conscious of the costs of their salary budgets.'

What are PRP's effects on pay costs?
- PRP seems to be self-financing in most cases.
- Some believe that PRP provides better value for money by encouraging better performance.
- Others, however, find it difficult to assess PRP's impact on the overall salary bill.

Do budgets constrain PRP's proper distribution?

Few organizations have 'forced distributions', limiting the percentage of employees who receive each assessment grade so that, for instance, only 5 per cent are rated 'outstanding', 15 per cent as 'highly effective', and so on. But most interviewees recognized that the budgeted salary bill acted as a constraint on the overall distribution (so that managers might be reluctant to put too many in the top assessment grade because that would result in their having to put more than they would like in the lower grades), and many interviewees from the private sector said that in practice a typical distribution emerged each year. For example, one organization's 'normal distribution' was

40–50 per cent in 'fully acceptable' (the second category) and 20 per cent in 'above standard'.

However, 'Robbing Peter to pay Paul' was reported to be a problem in one public-sector organization and was seen 'not to be fair' by the interviewee there. 'If you think about it, it's actually penalizing a division that might be performing extremely well. You might have got a group of people who are performing extremely well, all would be entitled to get the top increase, but you couldn't actually pay them all that.'

Consequently, very few people were receiving the top grade of PRP, which was causing 'a lot of frustration'. In this regard public-sector managers compared their treatment unfavourably with that which they thought happened in the private sector. As the manager quoted above confirmed, 'There is a fair bit of frustration around, because it's actually seen as penalizing the high performers. And also the actual percentages are really quite low. You can be flogging yourself to death and end up with a fairly low percentage, compared to outside industries.' The survey of Inland Revenue staff showed that 74 per cent of respondents believed that 'Staff are frequently denied the box marking they deserve because of a quota system'.

Do budgets constrain PRP's proper distribution?
- Few organizations have forced distributions, but in most the budgeted salary bill acts as a constraint.
- In most organizations, however, a typical distribution emerges each year. Target distributions may help to achieve consistency between managers.

How closely is PRP linked with performance management systems?

In her chapter on PRP in the IPM book on performance

management (Neale, 1991) Vicky Wright says, 'Even the most ardent supporters of PRP recognize that it is extraordinarily difficult to manage well.' The issues highlighted in this chapter reinforce that view. They suggest, moreover, that in many cases there has been insufficient clarity about the aims and objectives of PRP, that schemes have not always been drawn up with sufficient care or forethought, and that more attention needs to be paid to evaluation and monitoring. Moreover, not all modern management theory points so unequivocally to PRP as its proponents often imply. The theories underlying Deming's quality management (Scherkenbach, 1990) and the Harvard School's version of human resource management (Beer et al., 1984; Kanter, 1990) both advise against PRP, as well as against over-emphasizing pay and its link with 'successful' performance. Some modern psychology's emphasis on the importance of goal setting in performance may suggest that better results may be achieved without the frustration and potential demotivation of PRP, that is, with a high basic rate plus well specified targets (Locke et al., 1991).

Relatively few organizations put PRP in the context of performance management systems (PMS), which emphasize objective-setting and formal appraisal. Yet there is evidence, most notably from a survey carried out for the IPM by the Institute of Manpower Studies (Bevan and Thompson, 1991), that 'in terms of the effectiveness of peformance-related pay, respondents perceived it to be more effective when sitting alongside policies to manage employee performance, either as part of a PMS or as part of a more general approach. . . . There was also some evidence that performance management could be effective when not linked to PRP.' This raises the question of whether PRP is actually necessary to improve performance: might not other policies associated with PMS be enough to achieve this without PRP? The issue is echoed in one of the conclusions of the Inland Revenue survey,

'that very many staff feel they are already working to the
right standard and that they cannot improve. This may or
may not be true but, if it is untrue, it would seem that
management has to do much more than merely offer cash.'

Monitoring and evaluation
Linked with the lack of clarity about the objectives and
impact of schemes is the limited nature of attempts at
monitoring and evaluation. Monitoring of schemes con-
sists largely of attempting to achieve consistency between
the ratings of particular managers. As we have seen, few
organizations appear to have evaluated the schemes formally, or to have carried out employee attitude surveys
specifically targeted at the functioning of PRP. Attitude
surveys which ask the sort of questions listed on pp. 86–7
seem essential, not only to assess how well PRP is working
but also to provide information to enable schemes to be
adjusted. It appears that boards of directors and senior
managers rarely take time out to look at how their PRP
schemes are functioning. Instead personnel managers
seem to rely on routine discussions and inferences from
the data they collect as part of pay and appraisal processes
to gain a sense of how PRP is working. With certain
exceptions, this seems to cause them to have positive
views on the effectiveness of PRP, although in many cases
they also have qualifications and reservations.

PRP is often linked with the introduction of objective-
setting through the appraisal system. Yet little serious note
is taken of the fact that it may be easy to set objectives and
tasks to be completed, whereas assessing their impact or
effectiveness may not be so easy. One interviewee talked of
his firm moving to rewarding on achievement, not effort.
But, in the PRP scheme just set up in that company,
insufficient attention had been paid to clarifying output
measures. In accepting the basic principle of setting
objectives many managers seem to avoid or ignore the
question of how achieving these objectives really im-

pinges on overall organizational performance: it is often easier to measure inputs than outputs, actions rather than effectiveness. An example from social work makes the point: 'It's easier to work out how many visits a social worker makes than the quality of life of the people who get the visits.'

In some cases the main justification offered for PRP is that it makes managers take appraisal and the related (often newly introduced) system of objective-setting seriously. In this, PRP seems to have been relatively successful. Nonetheless it is difficult to achieve true objectivity in appraisal, and the 'blue-eyed boy' effect may always be a problem. As the Inland Revenue survey suggested, in the context of pay, what people *believe* to be true is perhaps the most important factor in influencing attitudes and behaviour. Some organizations are taking measures to maximize objectivity in appraisal through training and by reviewing and monitoring completed appraisals. Other organizations, it is clear, could do more in this respect.

The great majority of interviewees believed that the sort of problems described above were not inherent to PRP but very much a matter of its appropriateness to the type of organization, and illustrated the need to design systems properly. The widespread commitment to PRP implies that effort in many organizations in the next few years will not be spent on introducing alternative pay systems, but rather on improving and perfecting the working of PRP, with emphasis on improving objective-setting and the appraisal process. Observation of many of the objectives being set thus far suggests that managers, especially when setting them for people other than top management, tend to put all elements of the person's job in the statement of objectives without prioritizing them adequately; the failure of a lot of managers is that they are not prepared to leave anything out.

Improving performance-related pay
The evidence suggests that those organizations which
have put PRP into an effective performance management
system may well be setting more valid and precise
objectives. Managers could, though, be advised to ask
themselves whether they are really measuring 'contribution' and what in PRP is being measured. Is it inputs or
outputs or a mixture of both? And are the output measures
being used as proxies for input/effort or as an end in
themselves? Also, given that managers are concerned with
PRP as a message sender, more attention might be paid to
whether it is in fact giving mixed messages and how, if
indeed it is doing so, more consistent messages might be
achieved.

Organizations could perhaps also benefit from paying
more attention in their personnel planning to the bulk of
their employees who fall in the large middle group in
terms of motivation and performance. The emphasis in
managers' minds in designing payment systems (as well as
during the interviews) was very much on the two ends of
the spectrum – the high-flyers and the poor performers.
This lack of differentiation suggests that managers ought to
assure themselves that their PRP schemes are doing more
than rewarding the already motivated and demotivating
further the poorly motivated.

A deeper assessment and clarification of the objectives
and assumptions underlying payment systems might also
be helpful, even if the priority is to improve upon PRP
rather than to develop alternatives. Managements need to
have sufficiently targeted objectives when designing payment systems; to discuss fully the role they think either
money or the payment system can play, or which they
want them to play, in their organizational design; to clarify
whether they see PRP as the major lever of change; and to
assess whether in their organizations it can be relied on in
itself to effect cultural change. There are a host of dilemmas in designing payment systems. The fact that they

cannot always be resolved should not mean that they should not be faced. It is not enough to say somewhat dismissively, 'Too bad,' if people feel, for example, frustrated when the amount of money dependent on performance is increased and large differentials emerge which are felt to be unfair.

Expectancy theory stresses the importance of a series of links between behaviour and the rewards for that behaviour. For there to be a heightened motivation to perform, people:

- Have to feel able to change their behaviour.
- Have to feel confident that a change in the behaviour would reliably produce the rewards.
- Have to value the rewards sufficiently to justify the change in behaviour.

The links between behaviour and the rewards for that behaviour need to be spelled out more explicitly, so as to attempt to underpin the payment system with the legitimacy of a performance management system which is perceived to be fair.

It does seem that many of the dilemmas underlying PRP are not always being faced, either before introducing PRP schemes, or as part of their on-going maintenance. The problem of lack of evaluation may then go deeper than the fact that managers cannot clearly and unequivocally point to PRP bringing about desired changes. It may mean, especially as the objectives behind PRP may not be clear in the first place, that almost any 'feedback' can be perceived positively, since managers fit it into their frameworks in such a way as usually to introduce favourable judgements. More fundamentally it means, despite lip service increasingly being paid to the fit between human resource practices and the overall business strategy, that managers are clearly not assessing whether PRP can be improved – although it is only through evaluation that the dimensions of the fit can be judged and continually reappraised. It is not too early to expect attempts at objective assessment of the efficacy of PRP, given, as the present survey showed, that around a third of the schemes for non-manuals have been in existence for ten years or more.

How closely is PRP linked with performance management systems?
- Few organizations put PRP in the context of performance management, which emphasizes objective-setting and formal appraisal, or have seriously attempted to monitor PRP schemes.
- More could be done to assess and improve the effectiveness and objectivity of objective-setting and appraisal systems, and to look at the efficacy of PRP schemes.

Main lessons

- Money is not the only or even a major motivator. Other management tools need to be used, including in particular objective-setting and other measures associated with performance management.
- But it can be difficult to set measurable and realistic targets (especially if they are non-financial), and to achieve consistency between managers.
- Properly conducted appraisal is essential for PRP, but training in appraisal and regular and continuing monitoring and evaluation are required to ensure consistency and avoid discrimination against particular groups.
- Various measures, including attitude surveys and statistical analysis, need to be employed more widely to assess how well PRP schemes are working and to enable them to be adjusted. Schemes not only need to be fair, they need to be seen to be fair.

6

Planning pay better

The evolution of pay systems

In the opening chapter it was suggested that changes in the competitive environment were driving changes in pay schemes, and six possible aims of pay systems were suggested:

- Increasing organizational effectiveness.
- Helping organizations to compete in the labour market.
- Encouraging quality improvements.
- Helping to support desirable cultural change.
- Promoting communication and co-operation.
- Encouraging the development of skills and their flexible use.

Table 13 looks at the relationship between the different types of pay systems considered in this book and their likely effectiveness in each of these areas.

The main justification for using *traditional individual PBR schemes* is to increase effort and therefore production by rewarding employees for output. When output was the sole measure of success, individual PBR schemes seemed to meet the need. However, individual piece rate is now widely acknowledged to discourage attention to quality and 'right first time' attitudes. In some cases it is also being abandoned as part of a process of cultural change which encourages individual responsibility for performance and promotes the idea of continuous improvement. 'With every pair of hands a brain comes free,' as one manager put it. Individual PBR seems to discourage the promotion and acquisition of skills, because more money can often be earned doing a single repetitive job than working flexibly. So far as its effectiveness in labour market terms is

Table 13 Effects of pay systems on key organizational objectives

Effect on	Individual PBR	Group PBR	Profit-sharing	PRP
Effort	Positive in principle	Positive in principle	Little or no effect	Yes – for some
Recruitment and retention	Some employees like PBR; some don't; overall negative?	Neutral	Slightly positive	Some employees expect PRP
Quality	Can be negative	Depends on scheme; neutral to positive	Neutral	Depends on objectives set
Cultural change	Negative	Neutral	Slightly positive	Can be strongly positive
Co-operation	Negative	Positive within the group	Neutral to slightly positive	Depends on objectives; can be negative
Skills/ flexibility	Neutral to negative	May encourage flexibility, depending on scheme	Neutral	Not clear; depends on objectives set

concerned, there is some evidence from work carried out by NEDO (1991) in the clothing industry that labour retention is improved when individual PBR is taken out and replaced by team working.

Group-based PBR and other forms of output-related bonus have the advantage that they may encourage group performance and co-operation. They may, of course, emphasize departmental or sectional *esprit de corps* at the expense of the performance of the organization as a whole, but that depends on the size of the bonus and the measure or objective used.They may have slightly positive effects on skills, flexibility and quality, again depending on the rules of the scheme.

Profit-sharing in its various forms can highlight company performance. (Ironically, the effect may be most evident when the firm is doing badly and bonuses fall.) The obvious aim of such schemes is clearly a cultural one, saying to employees, in effect, 'You are part of this organization, its success or failure depends to a large degree on you, and therefore we will relate some of your remuneration to our profitability.' But the evidence seems to be that in reality profit-sharing has relatively little cultural impact, and its impact on the other areas referred to in Table 13 is probably more or less neutral.

PRP has received most attention in this book because it is relatively new. The PRP schemes that were introduced during the 1970s, and which spread broader and deeper in the 1980s, are widely supported by those who operate them. That PRP succeeds in motivating people may be open to question, but to varying degrees it does, for example, reward merit, assist processes of cultural change and convey messages about performance requirements. However, relative to the significance of the change, little thought seems to have been given to the processes by which PRP works. Confusion about the reasons for the introduction of PRP is one effect of this uncertainty. Is it brought in to reward, to motivate, or to change culture? The mechanisms by which it is supposed to operate and the effects on average performers in particular do not appear to have been thought through clearly. PRP on its own is not enough. To respond, people need to have sufficient control over the way they work. And they need to understand how to improve their effectiveness at work.

Moreover, there appears to be insufficient focus on the risks and potential problems involved in introducing PRP systems. In particular there is a lack of critical evaluation. Although some interviewees were asking questions like 'How well is it working?' and 'Is it having the desired effect?' very few were using tools like employee attitude surveys to provide answers they could trust. Too many simply said something to the effect that their judgement was based on faith. And less consideration than might have been expected seems to have been given to the question 'Are there ways of achieving what we want other than through the pay system?', for instance by making greater use of other approaches to performance management.

The search for an all-purpose pay system

The shift to PRP seems to have happened quickly, particularly among managers, but perceptions of the pace of change may be affected by the focus on schemes which change rather than the ones which do not. New approaches to pay fade in and out rather than happen overnight. PRP was already in substantial use before the 1980s had begun, but the speed of change accelerated in the 1980s. However, many systems fail to change long after they have outlived their usefulness, perhaps because of conservatism or because there is an element of 'better the devil you know'. For these reasons, at any given time in an organization of reasonable size, there may be several pay systems in operation. Individual PBR is being abandoned gradually. PRP, applied first to senior management, is now being extended further down the hierarchy. In this it is crucially different from other types of pay system. Unlike (for example) individual PBR, which was never seen as something that could form the basis of a pay system which would spread across the whole of an organization, PRP is seen by some to have that sort of versatility. Our findings call into question whether the 'Holy Grail' approach to the development of pay systems is correct, and whether PRP is indeed an all-purpose pay system.

If PRP had been found to be working more or less equally well in all the six areas suggested in Table 13, its diffusion across the field might be valid, but there are a number of reasons for raising doubts about the general applicability of PRP. There is the question of individual motivation, where PRP arrangements may now be seen to be, at least, 'not proven' in terms of effectiveness. There are also questions to answer about the size of bonuses, which, if they were large enough to motivate, would cause considerable hardship were the bonus to be withdrawn. There is a conundrum to be faced when, through no fault of individuals or the organization as a whole, hard times occur. On the one hand there is the logic that suggests that employees who participate in a bonus scheme when times are good ought to be prepared to forgo the bonus when times are lean. On the other hand there is the argument that more effort is needed when times are lean than when times are good, and that the withdrawal of a bonus can therefore have a negative effect. It may be that some way of reconciling these apparently contrary arguments is required. In any case, the universality of money as a motivator is in doubt. Whereas some people are motivated mainly by money, it is not true of many others.

Organizations comprise many groups of people carrying out different functions who have different standards and motivations. For some, operating very much as individuals, PRP may be the best approach. For others, group arrangements may be much better. In some cases incentives may still be appropriate, and group arrangements can be 'negotiated' with the people concerned so that objectives, rewards and risks are properly understood. For yet other groups, bonus arrangements may turn out to be demotivating and divisive. For them, a time-rated or straight salary system may be preferable and should not be thought of as a second-best option.

Looking at the relationship between cash flow and bonus payments, a clear distinction should perhaps be drawn between organizations which have a constant income – or at least one which is not subject to cyclical fluctuation – and organizations which are operating in the market and which make a profit or loss. In the latter case, if great confusion is not to be caused, it may be a good thing to separate payments under cyclical profit-related bonus schemes from payments under performance-related pay.

Finally, it seems likely that many of the organizations which have gone down the PRP route will be reviewing their scheme during the 1990s. (Many may be stimulated to do so earlier rather than later because of the effects of the recession on bonus payments.) How many will decide that it is too difficult to maintain, at the same time, objectives-based performance management arrangements and objectives-based performance-related pay? The difficulties this link causes in the operation of appraisal schemes, and the potential for undermining the processes of skill and competence development by reducing the amount of frankness in such discussions, may mean that it is preferable to separate the processes formally. (There seems to be no reason why the incentive of accelerated progress on a salary scale should not be built into an objectives-based performance management system, whilst an appraisal-based development process for individuals is run entirely separately.)

Developing a thoroughgoing approach to evaluation

Those responsible for managing how people are paid are increasingly aware of the contradictions and the tensions which may result as new systems are introduced and old ones are modified. Every pay system has plusses and minuses, and none will ever be completely fair. The important thing is for managers to be aware of the various features of each system, to understand the workings of the systems they employ and to seek to accentuate the positive and to minimize the negative. Given this need for pay system 'health checks', a major concern is the infrequency of evaluation of pay systems. Without information and analysis it is impossible to do more than guess at the effectiveness of individual pay systems.

The sort of information which was gleaned by the London School of Economics researchers who examined the attitudes of those covered by the Inland Revenue PRP scheme would be enormously valuable to other employers. As the experiences of the one company we found conducting attitude surveys of the people covered by their PRP system illustrates, these can be used to improve the processes of performance management and appraisal.

If the six tests set out in Table 13 are the most important output-related ways in which pay systems can be judged, there are certain house-keeping requirements which also need to be met:

- *Pay systems should work harmoniously with appraisal, performance management and other systems* which relate to and influence the performance of individuals and groups. Inconsistencies and contradictions between the parts can significantly undermine the effectiveness of a total package of management and motivational practices and policies.
- *Standards should be evenly and equitably applied* across the organization. What appears to be a fair system will be seriously undermined if it is not consistently applied. Some means of testing its application is necessary. One approach is to look at the dispersion of payments within the system. Others are to test by attitude surveys, and to use exit interviews and focus groups. Employees' views need to be taken fully into account; what managers think their employees believe is not a sufficient basis for evaluation. A particular concern is the possibility, for reasons which are initially difficult to control, that the distribution of bonus

payments is not reflecting the need for evenhandedness in the assessment of men and women. The possibility of an equal opportunities claim is something which will need to be avoided, but the need for fairness, and therefore effectiveness, ought to be a more pressing reason for eliminating bias against particular groups within the work force.

- *There needs to be a way of assessing the 'fall-out' effects* of pay systems. Individual PBR and PRP are unlikely substantially to improve team working. The question is whether they are having a harmful effect on team working. There needs to be some way of taking the temperature on such issues. Again, attitude surveys and exit interviews, for example, can help.

The key questions arising from the above discussion are, perhaps, 'What contribution can the pay system make to overall business success?' and 'How do we integrate pay into the overall business strategy?'. Insufficient numbers had thought about or installed other measures to reinforce the pay system. Few organizations had a coherent performance management strategy, even though theory and common sense suggest that a performance management system needs to be in place before PRP is introduced. The evaluative questions set out in Appendix 1 may help those responsible for pay systems to clarify their aims and to develop the right approach.

The relative lack of rigour all too often found in the preparation of schemes, and the absence of evaluation, may represent weaknesses which could undermine organizations' approach to pay. While there may be an element of truth in the view expressed by one interviewee that 'The best payment system is the one that's just been put in', managers should not be relying purely on novelty to achieve their desired goals.

Appendix 1

A checklist for evaluating and revising incentive pay systems

How should business goals link with the pay system?

- First decide what the business wants of its people, unit by unit and group by group.
- Communicate targets down through the organization.
- Make sure that messages about the business (e.g. quality, 'right first time', customer care) are reflected in the workings of the pay system.

What should the pay system seek to achieve?

- Would pay incentives increase motivation? Consider everyone, not just high-flyers or poor performers.
- How could the pay system help to improve recruitment and retention?
- What effect should the pay system have on quality and continuous improvement of products, services and processes?
- How might the pay system support the culture of the organization, and any desired cultural change?
- Does the pay system need to encourge co-operation and teamwork?
- How might the pay system encourage the acquisition and flexible use of skills?
- Are there alternative or complementary ways of achieving these objectives? Should use of the pay system be a fundamental part of the approach? What additional measures should be taken to reinforce the messages given by the pay system?

Who should be covered by incentive payments?

- Only those groups and individuals where there is a direct and quantifiable link between effort and output? Or more widely?
- How appropriate are individual incentives where team working is important?
- What sort of people does the organization currently employ, or want to employ in the future? Those who are largely motivated by money, or those who get their main motivation in other ways?

How much of pay should be at risk?

There is no final answer, but in designing a pay system it is worth thinking about:

- The need for motivation, group by group.
- The extent to which incentives can be strictly related to effort.
- Whether separate provision needs to be made to allow pay movements as market circumstances fluctuate.
- What the pay system is seeking to achieve. For example, the amount at risk may need to be relatively large if the aim is to motivate; smaller if it is to reward achievement.

How can incentive systems be made to work fairly and effectively?

- First make sure that performance management systems are effective.
- Ensure that personal objectives are fair and relevant to required performance.
- Broaden objectives if team working or interdepartmental co-operation is required.
- Ask employees and ask trade union representatives to get feedback on effectiveness and consistencies.

- Use attitude surveys and exit interviews to monitor employees' views. Don't just rely on managers' views.
- Don't forget to keep payments competitive in the external labour market.
- Be careful to treat men and women equally.
- Train managers to appraise properly and monitor markings to ensure consistency.
- Realize that introducing incentives is insufficient, on its own, to change culture and behaviour.

What about risks and problems?

- Don't risk demotivating the majority by implying that their work is unsatisfactory. Remember, most people think they are better than average. Most people will need to receive some performance payment.
- Consider whether personal appraisal and development can be separated from incentive pay to avoid undermining appraisal systems.
- Watch total costs (including the cost of monitoring) and control performance pay budgets.
- Relate objectives to criteria which avoid emphasizing short-term results at the expense of long-term success.

What mechanisms are there for review and evaluation?

- Is the board involved in the process?
- Continually monitor output measures, input costs, employee attitudes and management views in order to make improvements to the system.
- Circumstances change, so keep objectives under review during the year.
- Don't forget to reassess the pay system's contribution to overall business objectives.
- It is easy to say, 'Incentives work,' without knowing why!

Appendix 2

Methodology and sample of the IPM/NEDO survey

Methodology

A nation-wide postal questionnaire survey was conducted among 1,000 UK organizations across a wide cross-section of industries and services in both the private and the public sectors. The target sample consisted of three sub-samples, drawn as follows:

- A stratified random sample of 535 small, medium and large organizations drawn from the Kompass Industrial Database.
- A stratified random sample of ninety public-sector organizations in local government and health, drawn from the 1990 *Municipal Yearbook*.
- A random sample of 375 organizations drawn from the membership database of the IPM Compensation Forum, yielding a mix of industries and services which included some from the public sector, effectively increasing this particular sample to 100 organizations.

Response rate

Of the 1,000 questionnaires sent out, 372 were returned. In addition nineteen letters were received giving reasons for non-participation, and a further fifteen questionnaires were returned 'Unknown at this address', giving an overall response of 40 per cent, albeit an effective response rate of 39 per cent. Twelve returned questionnaires were unusable, rendering a final survey population of 360 organizations.

Survey sample

More than 75 per cent of the survey organizations were
from the private sector; 24 per cent had 500 or fewer
employees, 21 per cent over 10,000, with those employing
between 1,001 and 5,000 being disproportionately represented (29 per cent). Respondents were asked to indicate
whether their contribution represented a total organization, group, division, establishment or site. Approximately half were from total organizations, with groups
being the least represented (12 per cent). The majority of
establishments had no more than 500 employees, 41 per
cent having fewer than 250.

The manufacturing and service sectors were almost
equally represented, but, within the private-sector service
industries, the financial and business services were domi-
nant (16 per cent). The distributive trades, transport and
communication were under-represented, with only 7 per
cent of the total survey population. The majority of the
manufacturing industries were represented by groups,
divisions and establishments.

As might be expected, the participating public-sector
organizations were the biggest employers of manual workers, employing roughly 600,000-plus compared with
195,000-plus in the private sector.

Appendix 3

Members of the IPM/NEDO Incentive Pay Steering Group

Chairman

Michael Armstrong.

Members

Dr Alex Bowen, Head of Policy, Analysis and Statistics, Economics and Statistics Division, NEDO.
Michael Cannell, Manpower Adviser, NEDO.
Richard Coles, Head of Human Resources, Christian Salveson plc.
Colin Cummings, Assistant Secretary, Economic Department, Trades Union Congress.
Robbie Gilbert, Director of Employment Affairs, Confederation of British Industry.
Phil Long, Manager – Research, IPM.
Ken Mayhew, Pembroke College, University of Oxford.
Steve Palmer, former Assistant Director – Development, IPM.
John Stevens, Head of Manpower Division, NEDO.
Steve Williams, Director of Human Resource Development, ICL plc.
Dr Stephen Wood, Senior Lecturer, Department of Industrial Relations, London School of Economics.

Glossary

Appraisal-related pay. A method of payment whereby an employee receives increases in pay based wholly or partly on the regular and systematic assessment of job performance, conducted in the context of pre-set objectives.

Group payment by results (group PBR). Under this system, bonus pay is divided among members of a group or team, either equally or in an agreed ratio.

Incentive pay. A generic term covering types of pay systems which encourage effort and output and which are the subject of this book. They include all the types of system referred to in this glossary, except for incremental pay, time rates and skills-based pay. See also the discussion in Chapter 1.

Incremental pay. The traditional method of paying non-manual workers, under which salary increases automatically every year by set amounts until the individual reaches the top of the scale.

Individual payment by results (individual PBR). This may take many forms, some of them quite complex, but what they all have in common is that part of the employee's earnings is based directly on his or her personal performance, usually the level of output achieved (but sometimes the amount of time saved) by the individual over a set period, say a week. (Usually employees on individual PBR are paid partly by time rate, partly on the basis of their performance.) Most individual PBR schemes apply to manual workers, and performance is expressed in work study terms, with standard performance times based on

121

the 'rate of output which qualified workers can achieve without over-exertion as an average over the working day or shift provided they adhere to the specified method and provided they are motivated to apply themselves to their work' (British Standards Institution, *Glossary of Terms used in Work Study and Organisation & Methods*, BR 3138, revised 1979, London, BSI). However, there are some non-production jobs where individual PBR can be applied. For example, the commission paid to sales staff is a form of individual PBR.

Measured daywork (MDW) contains some of the elements of both the time rate and PBR systems. Pay is fixed at a higher rate than management would normally pay to a time-rate worker, on the understanding that the employee maintains a specific level of performance. Work measurement is used to set the required level and monitor the actual level.

Merit pay. Sometimes used simply as an alternative term to performance-related pay (PRP), but in this book is taken as a form of PRP in which the performance pay element is derived from an assessment by a manager which does not relate to the achievement of pre-set objectives.

Performance-related pay (PRP). A term sometimes used to cover a variety of reward arrangements, including those linked to company performance (profit-related pay), but in this book it means objectives-based appraisal-related pay (even if the performance review is separate in time from the pay review) or merit pay.

Piecework. The employee is paid at a specific rate (or price) per unit of output (i.e. per piece). It is the simplest form of individual PBR.

Plant/enterprise-wide bonus schemes differ from group

PBR in that they are based on the achievement of productivity targets set for a whole plant, site or unit. The total bonus is divided among all production members or employees on the same basis rather than by ratio.

Profit-related pay. A generic term for profit-sharing and share option schemes, which are based on organizational performance, employees receiving annual cash or share bonuses, including employee share options, based on the profit made in the previous accounting year.

Skills-based pay. Under this system, employees receive compensation for the range, depth and types of skills they possess. They are paid for the skills they are capable of using, not for the job they are performing at any particular point in time.

Time rates. Flat-rate pay, which is usually expressed as an hourly rate, a weekly wage, or an annual salary. In some PBR schemes time rates are used as the fall-back provision when, for whatever reason, an employee fails to meet a minimum standard of performance.

Note. The above definitions, except for those of incentive pay, incremental pay, merit pay, performance-related pay and skills-based pay, are based on those in ACAS advisory booklets No. 2, *Introduction to Payment Systems*, and No. 14, *Appraisal-related Pay*.

Bibliography

ADVISORY CONCILIATION AND ARBITRATION SERVICE. *Labour Flexibility in Britain*. London, ACAS, 1987. (ACAS Reports, 4.)

— *Developments in Payment Systems: the 1988 ACAS Survey*. London, ACAS, 1990. (Occasional Papers, 45.)

— *Introduction to Payment Systems*. London, ACAS, 1985. (Advisory Booklets, 2.)

— *Appraisal-related Pay*. London, ACAS, 1990. (Advisory Booklets, 14.)

ARMSTRONG, Michael, and MURLIS, Helen. *Reward Management: a Handbook of Remuneration Strategy and Practice*, second edition. London, Kogan Page in association with the Institute of Personnel Management, 1991.

BEER, M., SPECTOR, B., LAWRENCE, P.R., MILLS, P.Q., AND WALTON, R.E. *Managing Human Assets*. New York, Free Press; London, Collier-Macmillan, 1984.

BEVAN, Stephen, and THOMPSON, Marc. 'Performance management at the crossroads', *Personnel Management*, 23(11), November 1991, pp. 36–9.

BROWN, Wilfred B.D. *Piecework Abandoned: the Effect of Wage Incentive Systems on Managerial Authority*. London, Heinemann, 1962.

CASEY, B., LAKEY, J., COOPER, H., AND ELLIOTT, J. 'Payment systems: a look at current practice', *Employment Gazette*, August 1991, pp. 453–8.

CONFEDERATION OF BRITISH INDUSTRY. *Incentive Payments*. London, CBI, 1985.

HIBBETT, Angelica. 'Employee involvement: a recent survey', *Employment Gazette*, December 1991, pp. 659–64.

INCOMES DATA SERVICES LTD. *IDS Report*, Nos. 392–565. London, IDS, various years.

— *Guide to Incentive Payment Schemes*. London, IDS, 1980.

— *Incentive Bonus Schemes*. London, IDS, 1989. (Studies, 443.)

— *Paying for Performance*. London, IDS, 1988. (Research Files, 9.)

— *Profit-related Pay*. London, IDS, 1990. (Studies, 471.)

— *Bonus Schemes*, part 1. London, IDS, 1991. (Studies, 488.)

INVOLVEMENT AND PARTICIPATION ASSOCIATION. *How to Introduce Profit-related Pay*. London, IPA, 1991.

KANTER, R. *When Giants learn to Dance*. London, Unwin Hyman, 1990.

LABOUR RESEARCH DEPARTMENT. *Performance Appraisal and Merit Pay: a Negotiators' Guide*. London, LRD, 1990.

LOCAL AUTHORITIES CONDITIONS OF SERVICE ADVISORY BOARD. *Handbook on Performance-related Pay*. London, LACSAB, 1990. (PRP Reports, 2.)

— *Performance-related Pay in Practice: Case Studies from Local Government*. London, LACSAB, 1990. (PRP Reports, 3.)

— *Performance-related Pay in Practice: a Survey of Local Government*. London, LACSAB, 1990. (PRP Reports, 4.)

LOCKE, E.A., SHAW, K.N., SAARI, L.M., and LATHAM, G.P. 'Goal setting and task performance, 1969–1980', *Psychological Bulletin*, 90, 1991, pp. 125–52.

LONG, Phil. *Performance Appraisal Revisited*. London, IPM, 1986.

MARSDEN, David, and RICHARDSON, Ray. *Does Performance Pay Motivate? A Study of Inland Revenue Staff*. London, Inland Revenue Staff Federation, 1991.

MASON, Bob, and TERRY, Michael. *Trends in Incentive Payment Systems: into the 1990s*. Glasgow, University of Strathclyde, Department of Organisation, Management and Employment Relations, 1990. (Discussion Papers, 2.)

NATIONAL ECONOMIC DEVELOPMENT OFFICE. *Team Working: a Guide to Modular Manufacturing in the Garment Industries*. London, NEDO, 1991.

NEALE, Frances (ed.). *The Handbook of Performance Management*. London, IPM, 1991.

SCHERKENBACH, W.W. *The Deming Route to Quality and Productivity*. London, Mercury, 1990.

SMITH, I.G. *Incentive Schemes: People and Profits*, second edition, Kingston upon Thames, Croner, 1991.